THE ELUSIVE FORCE

A REMARKABLE CASE OF POLTERGEIST ACTIVITY AND PSYCHOKINETIC POWER

By Anna Ostrzycka and Marek Rymuszko

Translated by Joel Stern

Anomalist Books
Charlottesville, Virginia

CONTENTS

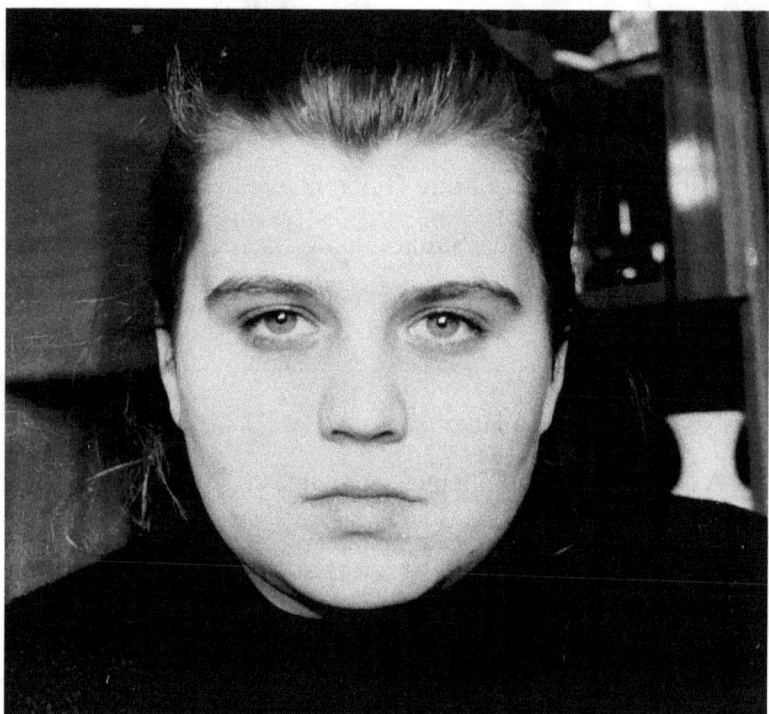

Photo of Joasia Gajewski by Szymon Polański, www.polanskistudio.pl

FOREWORD

Anomalous phenomena–strange happenings, if you will–are often the driving force behind scientific advances. It is the unusual event or the unexplained observation that causes scientists to wonder what is lacking in their understanding of the world that leaves the anomaly begging for an explanation.

Though science, in the abstract, may welcome anomalies, more often than not individual scientists are less than enthusiastic about them. For centuries scientists have been working hard to build up a coherent picture of the way the universe works, and they are not eager to have someone come along and tell them that something is wrong or incomplete with their picture. Often the first reaction to a particularly glaring anomaly is to deny it, or to attempt to explain it away using more conventional concepts.

The controversial branch of science known as parapsychology has been responsible for throwing up more than its share of anomalies–communication without sensory information (ESP), action at a distance (psychokinesis), among others. None of the anomalies with which parapsychology grapples is more baffling than the poltergeist. Indeed, the phenomena associated with poltergeist cases tax the "boggle threshold" of even the most open-minded scientist and lay person alike.

Cases such as the one you are about to read place one in an awkward position. Either you have to believe that a good number of trained scientists, medical personnel, and journalists are really liars or gullible fools (who, in addition, are willing to sacrifice their reputations by putting their names to the reports), or you must accept that they were witnesses to phenomena for which contemporary science has no explanations. Granted, we all encounter a sufficient number of liars and fools that we can be forgiven for succumbing to the temptation to dismiss what is in this book as nonsense. But would that really be fair? Would it be scientifically justified?

I shall leave it to you to decide if it is fair. Whether it is scientifically justified depends on how well the reports can be integrated with other findings on the same topic. Is it an isolated case, unlike anything else ever reported, or does it fit a pattern built up from similar, independent reports? If it is the former, then science would be justified in raising questions about the reliability of the reports. If it is the latter, then perhaps science should credit these reports and begin to look into the matter.

With poltergeist phenomena it is very much the latter situation. In fact, I hope you will not think me facetious if I say that the case of Joasia Gajewski is pretty typical stuff–for a poltergeist case, that is—though its duration places it among the longest on record. However incredible you may find the incidents related in this book, I can assure you that virtually all of them have precursors in the hundreds of similar cases that have been reported and investigated over the centuries. But Joasia's case may be one of the most interesting in decades.

We are nowhere close to having an explanation of what is happening in a poltergeist case. The best we can do is to continue to collect and study these reports in the hope that we may discover some new clues to both the psychology and the physics involved. To that end, this book is a valuable addition to the database.

— Richard S. Broughton, PhD*

* At the time Dr. Broughton wrote this Foreword in July of 1991 he was director of research at the Institute for Parapsychology in Durham, North Carolina.

Joasia (left) and her parents, Andrzej and Ewa Gajewski, in 1989 (credit Joel Stern).

Chapter 1
WHAT HAPPENED IN SOSNOWIEC IN 1983?

There is nothing remarkable about Plonow Street in Sosnowiec, Poland. It has many old houses, most of which date from before the war, and the families in that district have been residing there for twenty years or more.[1]

Andrzej and Ewa Gajewski and their thirteen-year-old daughter Joasia[2] occupied a studio apartment on the first floor of a building at 5 Plonow Street. The girl attended sixth grade in primary school no. 1 in Sosnowiec. Her mother was a telephone operator in a local office, her father a plumber employed at the Sosnowiec Steelworks. All in all, an average family, one of many who lived in the historical region known as Silesia.

On June 26, 1982, Maria Tomecki, Joasia's maternal grandmother, passed away. We note this event because psychological tests administered to the girl later on showed that she had been very close to her grandmother and was profoundly shaken by her death. It should also be mentioned that the youngster was then undergoing intense puberty-related hormonal changes.

But our story actually begins in 1983. At that time newspapers and magazines first featured stories about the young girl, Joasia Gajewski, in whose presence odd psychokinetic effects allegedly occurred. Unfortunately, most of the reports on these happenings were sensationist in tone, which effectively obscured the nature of the phenomenon and made it hard to separate fact from fiction. When we undertook to describe this phenomenon, we did not immediately accept it as real.

---

1   This book was written in 1986, except for the last two sections of the last chapter, "A Final Note."
2   Pronounced yo-AH-sha, accent on the second syllable. "Joasia" is a diminutive form of the name "Joanna" (such as "Joni" for "Joan" or "Johanna").

Accounts by Joasia's parents and other persons who came into contact with her during the several weeks prior to the outbreak of paranormal phenomena repeatedly mention that she "crackled." This sound resembled finger-snapping or clicking (the exact word used by our interviewees) concentrated around the teenager. The acoustical effects first occurred in mid-January 1983, according to one version of the story, or in early February, according to a second version. Little attention was paid to these sounds at the time; they were simply ascribed to static electricity from handling plastic articles, wearing woolen garments, etc. People would only joke that one had to be careful when shaking Joasia's hand, because lately she gave quite a "jolt."

Another circumstance that may or may not be important in determining the origin of the phenomenon is Joasia's illness at the time. From early March 1983 the girl had been down with the flu. She had a nagging cough and her temperature exhibited strange fluctuations. For example, it would inexplicably rise all of a sudden to 40°C (104°F), at least that is what the thermometer indicated, then fall and remain on a level close to normal. What's more interesting, a comparison of the thermometer reading with direct touch of the girl's body seemed to rule out such a high fever. The physicians who examined Joasia considered her influenza atypical; some of them suspected a contagious disease but could not find any of its tangible symptoms. The routine medical procedures and conclusions in this case can be attributed to the fact that in Sosnowiec, as in all of Silesia, children often suffer from bronchitis and other respiratory ailments because of the severe air pollution accompanying the region's heavy industry.

April 4, 1983, was the second day of the traditional Polish Easter festivities. It went by uneventfully in the Gajewski household, except that Joasia had felt worse since the morning, complaining of a persistent headache. After the family dinner, Andrzej left for his job on the night shift at the Sosnowiec Steelworks, while the girl, her mother, and her grandfather, Marian Tomecki, watched television. As it was late, Tomecki decided to spend the night with the Gajewskis and return home the following day. All three of them went to bed around midnight. The mother slept on a cot in the kitchen; Joasia and her grandfather, on a sofa bed in the parlor.

Everything began around three o'clock in the morning. It was then that a straw mat fell upon Marian Tomecki's head. Awakened, he tried to fasten it back onto the wall, but the mat "tore itself from his hands and danced around," he said. At first he thought Joasia was pulling a prank, only it turned out the girl was asleep.

A moment later, pandemonium ensued.

According to all three witnesses, various objects began flying through the air, mostly plates and glasses. Some of them, hurtling at tremendous velocity across the apartment, smashed into walls and a sideboard. Window panes rattled; furniture shook. Matches fluttered about as if thrown by an invisible hand. Afraid they might start a fire, Grandfather Tomecki chased them around the parlor and stomped on them. Once the light was turned on, the havoc did not stop. What was even more terrifying, fragments of shattered glassware, as if drawn by an uncanny force, flew at the girl and cut her. The blanket covering her was so charged with electricity that it gave off sparks.

With every passing moment the bedlam grew worse. The frightened mother, daughter, and grandfather fled to the couple living upstairs, Jan and Gertruda Jach, who had already been roused by the din on the first floor. Jan Jach, in fact, was the first outside observer of the psychokinetic effects. His statement below is presented on the basis of a tape recording we made in December 1983 while accompanying a Japanese television crew.

Q. Can you describe for us what was happening?
A. My wife and I were awakened by a tremendous commotion downstairs. It sounded like somebody was breaking dishes on the floor and pounding the wall with a heavy object. I thought the neighbor might've had too much to drink, maybe a family squabble was going on there. That really surprised me, because the Gajewskis were quiet people and such things never happened among them… I no sooner said that to my wife when Mrs. Gajewski ran up here with her daughter and father. They were scared to

death. They said things were flying around the apartment like the end of the world had come. They asked to stay with us for a while, since they were afraid to go back.

Q. What was your reaction?

A. I thought it was a dumb joke. I went down to the first floor with them. When I opened the door, I saw everything in the apartment was shattered. There was glass everywhere and dents in the walls. The place was in shambles.

Q. Was anything flying when you went down there?

A. Not then. We stood around a long time but nothing happened.

Q. In that case, did you only see the aftereffects or something else?

A. That was only when I came the second time.

Q. Tell us more about it.

A. When the racket downstairs started up again, I returned there and saw glasses, plates, pots, and lots of other objects smashing into the wall. The noise was unbelievable.

Q. You saw objects flying?

A. Not flying, only when they hit the wall. Nobody was in the room; Mrs. Gajewski and her daughter were standing with me in the doorway. Those dishes must've been flying incredibly fast, because you couldn't see them until they dropped.

Q. What did you do then?

A. Well, naturally I was scared. I didn't know what to think, so I hurried back upstairs with the Gajewskis.

Q. While the girl and her mother were in your apartment, did any objects move spontaneously?

A. Not at first, only later on.

Q. Exactly when was "later on?"

A. A few seconds afterwards. My wife made tea, and all of a sudden things began "acting up." The first object to fly was a book, which fell under the sideboard. Joasia Gajewski picked it up and put it on the desk, but a moment later it flew under the sideboard again. Nobody could have thrown it, as we were all sitting about ten feet away then.

Q. What else do you remember?

4

A. The girl looked ill and complained of a headache. Her mother said she probably had a fever. Her temperature was taken, and the thermometer showed 40.5C (104.9F). Then the girl dozed off and everything quieted down. [End of recording]

Alarmed by his wife's phone call, Andrzej Gajewski arrived home around four in the morning. He left work with great reluctance because it was difficult to break away from his shift at the plant, and besides, he thought his wife must have been imagining things. Once he reached the threshold of the apartment, however, he realized her story was true. When he returned with his family from the Jachs and opened the door, he immediately saw a stoneware pot fly from the kitchen into the parlor. It shattered the glass pane of the sideboard and then broke into pieces on the floor.

The next few days not only failed to bring a respite but witnessed an intensification of the phenomenon. Glass shards–the remnants of flying jars, tumblers, plates, mugs, bottles, etc. — had to be removed from the floor almost constantly. When the Gajewskis implored the local authorities, they were treated like lunatics or hoaxers. A physician from the emergency medical service who came to examine the feverish Joasia asked curtly who in the family was mentally ill and then departed, leaving the girl unconscious. At every step her parents met with distrust and hostility. The repeated cannonades in their apartment exasperated the neighbors, who were unable to sleep.

The turning point came when Andrzej Gajewski, after much effort, finally persuaded officers from a nearby police station to inspect the apartment. (They would later say they had also thought some kind of hoax was being perpetrated.)

The first evening went by uneventfully. The Gajewskis felt dejected. Fortunately, they managed to persuade Sgt. Tadeusz Slowik, the district constable, to come the next day. This time the effects (which were also witnessed by one of the neighbors) occurred fairly soon. A few minutes after Joasia returned from the doctor, all hell broke loose. Glasses, screws, and other items started flying about in trajectories contrary to the fundamental laws

5

of physics. For example, objects would zoom out of the kitchen, execute a sharp turn in the air, and land in the parlor or slam into the opposite wall. Some of them, in contrast to previous experience, were clearly visible in flight.

The police report, which stated unequivocally that inexplicable physical phenomena involving the spontaneous movement of objects were occurring in an apartment at 5 Plonow Street, convinced the municipal authorities to take the whole matter seriously. The Gajewskis were visited by the chief architect of Sosnowiec, Lech Fulbiszewski, accompanied by personnel from the Department of Urban Planning. As he rode down Plonow Street, engineer Fulbiszewski concluded that the kinetic effects in the apartment were being caused by the settling of the building's walls. In a region with dozens of underground mining galleries, such a hypothesis seemed quite plausible. This meant the people living there were in danger.

But an inspection of the building, which was some thirty to forty years old, failed to reveal any defects in its construction. Nor could any trace of cracks be found in the walls. At the same time, the officials present in the apartment witnessed phenomena they had known about only from hearsay. Fulbiszewski and his companions observed a jar of mustard and a bottle fly from the kitchen into the parlor, where they smashed against the wall. They also saw various objects leaping several feet around the apartment, as well as fragments of glass flying to the girl's hands from a considerable distance.

In view of this situation, the architect advised the municipal authorities that the Gajewskis would need other lodgings at once. This decision was also made personally by the deputy mayor of Sosnowiec, Jozef Stankiewicz, who subsequently gave his reasons for it in a press interview: "Of course we didn't take such an incredible story at face value. A police officer and a municipal government employee were posted in the Gajewskis' apartment around the clock. We saw with our own eyes that the reports had been true. Objects, particularly ones made of glass, really did move in the child's direction. If only out of concern for her health and safety, we felt obligated to do everything in our power to help those people."

This solicitude was in marked contrast to the often indiscreet media coverage of the happenings in the Gajewskis' apartment, particularly a television report that unconscionably divulged their exact address. The results were not long in coming. The building at 5 Plonow Street began attracting large crowds of sensation seekers who rang the doorbell and pounded on the windows, demanding to be let in. Exorcists, members of dubious sects, and psychics desiring to communicate with the spirit world also started flocking to Sosnowiec from every part of the country. The Gajewskis, who are Catholic but who have never ostentatiously professed their faith (neither their former nor present apartment had any devotionalia indicative of religious piety), decided to receive only the local parish priest, Father Jan Smok. At the family's request he offered up invocations in their "haunted" home, which failed, however, to alleviate the situation. This did not keep a journalist from claiming (and his story was repeated continually by gossips) that a mysterious force had knocked the aspergillum out of the priest's hand during his visit to the Gajewskis. Like many of the other highly exaggerated accounts, this was total nonsense.

Official confirmation by the municipal authorities that the strange physical phenomena occurring at 5 Plonow Street were real triggered a search for their mechanism and causes. After the hypothesis regarding the settlement of the building's walls was ruled out, radiesthesists were consulted. A representative of the Radiesthesia Association in Gliwice, Jadwiga Zborowski, opined that the observed effects were due to "heavy irradiation of the apartment by a watercourse running [...] along the wall that is the primary target of the flying objects." She also conjectured that Joasia Gajewski might be a kind of human generator amplifying the intensity of the radiation.

The radiesthesist's verdict, for lack of another explanation, was accepted with a feeling of relief. But this relief was short-lived; when the Gajewskis moved into the new apartment allocated to them in Czeladz outside of Sosnowiec, the phenomena followed them. What had been just a suspicion thus became a certainty. It turned out that watercourses had nothing to do with the kinetic effects occurring around the girl. This conclusion was borne out by the cessation of such phenomena in their Plonow Street studio apartment once the Gajewskis had left (the place remained empty for a long time, and is now occupied by other tenants). After only a few days in this new residence, however, the pandemonium resumed with broken dishes, hundreds of glass fragments embedded in the walls, shaking furniture, and spontaneous unscrewing of faucets.

We set ourselves the goal of recording the odd physical effects as fully and systematically as we could, in the belief this would give us a chance to perceive the patterns behind them. Our task proved to be formidable if not impossible.

First of all, we were unable to ascertain any correlations between the time of day and the spontaneous movement of objects. It happened both in the daytime and at night, whether the girl was asleep or engaged in her normal activities. Nor were the kinetic effects ever preceded (at least in the initial phase) by a distinct sound. Sometimes, but only sometimes, we could hear clicks resembling finger-snapping. It was also certain that Joasia had no conscious control over what transpired around her.

We likewise failed to discover any relationship between an object's material composition and its potential for spontaneous movement. According to eyewitness accounts, all manner of things would fly around the apartment—from dishes and flatware to screws, shoes, and a hairbrush.

Incidentally, there is an amusing story involving the hairbrush that may indicate a link between the girl's mental processes and the kinetic effects. Once when Joasia was sleeping, a brush on her nightstand zipped into the hallway, where it hit the wall and fell on the floor. When questioned later by a psychologist, the youngster said she had dreamt that night of going to a hairdresser, who gave her a lousy hairdo that really upset her.

Analysis of the flights themselves did not lead to any general conclusions. They usually occurred very quickly, so much so that nobody could see an object when it took off or while it was flying. The most that people perceived was a blurred shape, practically a streak, for a mere split second. Moreover, the concomitant acoustical effects were disproportionately loud relative to the mass, weight, and composition of the moving objects. The nature of these effects can best be illustrated by a comparison used by one of the witnesses. According to his account, a tumbler that smashed against a wall (and that must have flown in from the kitchen, since there were no glass objects in the room where he was sitting with the Gajewskis at the time) shattered with such a deafening bang that he thought the TV picture tube had exploded.

Some objects, however, did fly slowly and were perfectly visible, such as a cup of unfinished tea left in the kitchen. First it glided into Joasia's bedroom, leaving behind a trail of spilled liquid, then veered into the parlor.

As if this were not enough, some accounts contain details that defy analysis, e.g., the spontaneous unscrewing of faucets, the overturning of a heavy sewing machine that spun in circles, and the winding of the cord of an unoperated vacuum cleaner across the floor.

The routine medical examinations Joasia underwent in late May and early June 1983 proved inconclusive. Although the girl complained of health problems, particularly headaches, no tangible reason for them could be found. The mysterious temperature fluctuations also continued (in the course of one measurement, for example, it was necessary to use a bath thermometer because the scale on a common medical thermometer did not go high enough). During an EKG examination, the glass pane of the control panel of the apparatus suddenly cracked.

Unfortunately, most of the doctors who saw Joasia during this period treated her like a mentally unbalanced person or a hoaxer. This happened at a pediatric hospital where, upon completion of the tests, the patient and her parents were labeled delusional.

The case, it seemed, had reached an impasse.

Joasia with Dr. Eustachiusz Gadula, a member of the research team that studied the girl for a period of 40 months in 1983-1986.

Chapter 2
SHORT CIRCUITS, RESONANCES, FALSE STARTS

There is no telling what Joasia Gajewski's fate might have been if she had not come under the care of Dr. Eustachiusz Gadula, then head of the paraplegic ward at the Miners Medical and Vocational Rehabilitation Center No. 1 in Tarnowskie Gory. Thanks to his dedication, courage, and personal involvement, a scientific team consisting of specialists in various disciplines was assembled in May 1983. Disregarding the obstacles in their path and the not always favorable atmosphere, they assumed the task of investigating the phenomenon of the Sosnowiec teenager in its manifold biophysical, psychological, and medical aspects.

Before this took place, however, the girl drew the attention of scientists from the PBS (Polish Biocenotic Society), which was founded in early 1983 and included among its members engineers, physicists, architects, and physicians. This organization's name derives from the Greek "bios" (life), "keines" (united, joint), and "tikos" (done). Almost from the outset, the PBS delved into psychotronics and especially the alternative medical modalities such as bioenergy therapy.

When newspaper stories on Joasia Gajewski began generating widespread interest in the case, the PBS sent a team headed by Professor Lech J. Radwanowski to Czeladz in late April 1983. Assisted by a radiesthesist, they carried out the first tests and experiments with the youngster.

Members of the team attempted mainly to ascertain the "nature of the field emitted by the girl's body." They concluded it was "neither a magnetic, nor an electric, nor an electromagnetic field." (Later studies would show that this conclusion was unfounded or at any rate definitely premature.) Tests designed to measure the effect Joasia might have on the resistance of a wire and on the electrostatic field of condensers yielded negative results.

The next experiment aimed at determining the youngster's effect on various objects suspended from a string. The official report signed by the entire team stated that Joasia Gajewski, while holding her hand several centimeters away from those objects, was able to move them at will regardless of the type of material used (metal, wood, crystals, etc.). The commission also noted that when persons approached within 20 cm of the girl's outstretched arms they suddenly felt weak, as if they had lost a great deal of weight. This feeling was experienced by all those who conducted the experiment, but we should emphasize that it was purely subjective.

An important part of the studies carried out with Joasia was the so-called Manczarski Test,[3] in which a sender telepathically transmits geometric figures drawn on a piece of paper to a receiver. Out of the twelve figures transmitted, Joasia correctly guessed eight, much better than chance probability. When asked how she picked up the information sent to her, she replied that at the moment the tester was making a choice one of the figures on the card in front of her would "become larger, warmer, and more pleasant."

The greatest success achieved in the course of this initial research was Joasia's bending a stainless-steel spoon ninety degrees within six minutes, merely by rubbing it with two fingers of her right hand. Her bending of spoons and other metal items received much publicity and was repeated hundreds of times under various (including scientifically controlled) conditions. More on this later, but here we shall just note that although this was the first such experiment in which Joasia participated, it came off perfectly.

We had an opportunity to observe the second series of tests and experiments, which took place on May 30, 1983. We had gone to Czeladz several days after Mrs. Gajewski phoned us to

3   Margaret Moga, "Radio Waves Associated with Telepathy," *Natural Healing Waves*, September 26, 2020, https://www.naturalhealingwaves.com/telepathy-and-radiowaves.

say that her daughter's headaches and the accompanying kinetic effects were getting worse.

The basic experiment employed a prototype apparatus for measuring so-called functional potentials, invented by Dr. Ireneusz Janczarski of the Warsaw Academy of Medicine and by Dr. Jerzy Sosnowski. The device consisted of two vessels filled with an electrolyte solution, plus an electronic device for registering the difference in potentials between the fingers of both hands. Repeated measurements showed that the values of the potentials recorded by the apparatus at the moment the girl was hooked up to it were several times higher than for other people (in our case, for example, the values amounted to 5-10 units, whereas Joasia's ranged between 30 and 49).

This time the experiment involving the movement of objects on a string ended in failure. Also unsuccessful was a telepathy test we had prepared, similar to the one administered to Uri Geller at Stanford University (i.e., guessing the number of dots on the top side of a die placed inside a closed aluminum container). On the other hand, the spoon-bending experiment once again confirmed the girl's amazing powers. The first spoon was bent after some twenty minutes of gentle rubbing with two fingers. (Before the attempt, we had Joasia wash her hands so that there could be no possibility of her using a substance to "soften" the metal.) The second spoon took five minutes to bend; the angle of its curve was approximately 110 degrees. Thanks to the presence of Maciej Billewicz, a reporter from the Polish news agency Interpress, both experiments were photographed.

Let's consider for a moment the flatware bent by Joasia. The operative force here is clearly paranormal, since analogous tests with other people have been unsuccessful. The moment immediately preceding the final effect is of particular interest. It looks as though the spoon were bending in an arc or drooping like the broken calyx of a flower on the spot where Joasia rubs it. If one tried to obtain such an effect through a mechanical force the metal would snap on that spot, but the girl's "rubbing" inexplicably causes metal to "soften." This spot also seems to have a higher temperature, which is perceptible to the touch. (However, later experiments conducted at the Institute of Physics at Jagiellonian University, where the temperature of the material was measured immediately after the girl bent it, did not bear out this conclusion.) We should add that this experiment does not succeed with aluminum flatware, which breaks under Joasia's fingers.

On the basis of the aforesaid tests (which in retrospect, must be regarded as random and superficial, especially when compared with subsequent studies carried out by Dr. Gadula's team), the biocenotic researchers formulated a tentative working hypothesis to explain the phenomena occurring around the girl. In their view, this was an extremely rare case of "local disturbance of gravitational forces." In other words, Joasia Gajewski supposedly emits a peculiar field (energy) in which the law of gravity ceases to operate.

The media frenzy that arose when Joasia Gajewski first attracted public notice lasted nearly two months. Fortunately, it subsided and then faded away altogether. We say "fortunately," because among the plethora of news items covering her case in the spring of 1983 (the overwhelming majority of which were blatantly sensationalized), just a mere handful contributed anything worthwhile to knowledge of the weird phenomena seriously disrupting the Gajewskis' family life. Irrespective of their informational value, however, these items represent a sociological phenomenon in their own right and thus deserve attention, especially as some of the more important ones had an international impact.

The hypothesis formulated by the scientists of the Polish Biocenotic Society originally appeared in *Kurier Polski* on May 16, 1983. During the next few days, the editorial office of this popular daily was barraged with calls from around the world (so many, in fact, that the international switchboard short-circuited when reporters phoning simultaneously from Belgrade and London demanded an immediate connection).

The first to call were the Japanese. Kyotaka Hirai, phoning from Shodensha Publishing in Tokyo, inquired about sundry details: what the previous experiments had been, what color Joasia's hair and eyes were, whether she was short or tall, how she dressed, whether she liked to read or go to the movies, what her favorite subjects at school were, and whether all these odd happenings were affecting the youngster's grades and her relations with peers.

No sooner had the conversation with Tokyo ended when Japan rang up again, via the Warsaw office of Yomiuri Shimbun, the largest media conglomerate in Japan. This time the caller asked what would be the next scientific studies on Joasia. A Danish journalist with a Copenhagen evening paper expressed his great eagerness to follow the case and certainly take part in an experiment with the girl. A famed psychic called from Paris, offering to send her a package of clothing, particularly cotton garments. (A very sensible idea, incidentally, for it was obvious she ought to wear apparel that minimized static electricity.) A Czech paper carried a piece about the psychokinetic marvel by a Polish correspondent who had never been to Sosnowiec but had simply rewritten a colleague's article for his own use—and no doubt for his own financial gain. The Gajewski case was also featured in the Yugoslav *Ilustrovana Politika* and the British journal *Psychic News*.

Predictably the press began churning out sheer absurdities, such as one item in an American tabloid that described a four-year-old girl who "scampered around in pursuit of flying socks." The concocted story, which got Joasia's name right but nothing else, included a photograph, but it wasn't of her. What's worse, the author falsified remarks that he claimed were made to him by Silesian psychologist Miroslaw Harciarek. Dr. Harciarek, who actually had conducted tests and studies with the youngster, wondered for a long time where this fabrication originated, since he had not given an interview to anyone. It was not until later that he recalled mentioning his research project at a private social event during a stay abroad. Unfortunately, he could not have foreseen that one of the guests, a reporter, would take the liberty to distort and embellish overheard cocktail-party chatter.

All this was going on at a time when we were the only journalists among the very few people privy to the Gajewskis' new address in Czeladz. The curtain of secrecy—after the family's ordeals while they were still living on Plonow Street in Sosnowiec — proved to be a blessing, for it allowed them to finally enjoy a little peace and quiet, at least as far as unwelcome visitors were concerned.

Despite our best efforts, however, we were not always able to fend off intrusive newshounds. Once, for example, a group of Japanese reporters touring Prague insisted on seeing Joasia during their stay in Europe. Having obtained hard won permission, they shot a copious amount of film material and left quite satisfied. It is easy to imagine their dismay, therefore, when they found upon returning to Japan that their labor had been wasted — the film was unexposed! The reason for this remains unknown, but one thing is definitely true: often digital watch batteries discharged and radios and tape recorders malfunctioned around the teenager. A coincidence or something else? Not wishing to speculate, we will just say that a similar glitch occurred in our presence several months afterward (more about this incident later).

Frankly, our purpose for concealing the family's new address was not to artificially create some sort of information monopoly. Along with the research group, we simply came to realize that if the Sosnowiec phenomenon were to be studied with due scientific rigor, its media coverage should be stopped or at least tightly restricted. Joasia's parents, with nerves clearly strained to the limit, readily agreed.

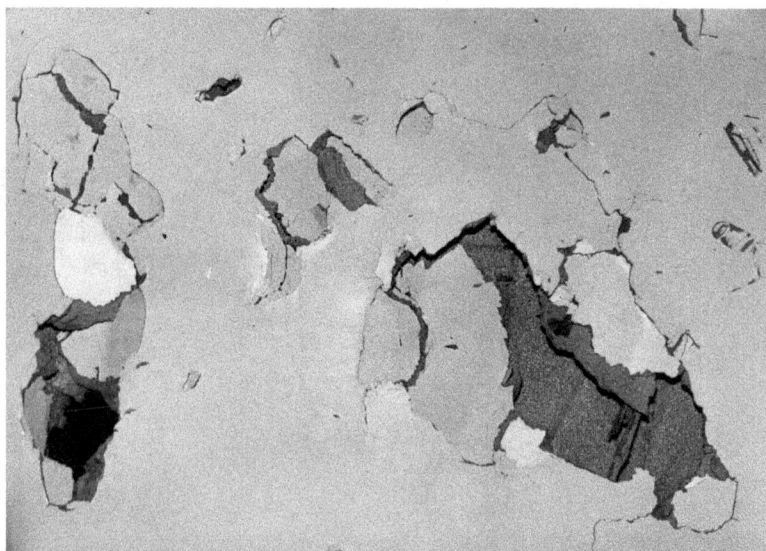

Damage visible in the front hallway of the Gajewskis' apartment.

Chapter 3
JUST LIKE US, ONLY A LITTLE DIFFERENT

Thus far we have devoted relatively little attention to Joasia herself, her milieu, the reactions of the people around her, and the girl's own attitude toward the phenomena she suddenly had to confront.

The reflections and insights we would like to share stem from our observation of Joasia over the course of several years and from the innumerable conversations we have had with her. They somewhat run ahead of certain things that crucially shaped later events, but failure to touch upon the general psychological and environmental factors that constitute the background of this story would inevitably detract from the value of our reporting and make it difficult to understand some of its important elements.

Let's begin by saying that Joasia (5'5", b. March 25, 1970), contrary to the common view we have often heard, is not demonic in the least. She is an average girl (with respect to the environment in which she was raised), easy-going, and attractive. When we first met her she appeared to be surprised and troubled by the situation in which she found herself. Eventually she grew accustomed to it, to the point where she began treating the phenomena besetting her as an inseparable and somewhat amusing part of everyday life.

Such an attitude undoubtedly facilitated her adaptation to what must be termed extraordinary conditions, but it also incurred criticism or suspicion that she was deliberately engaging in pranks. Yet this was never the case, for the girl herself usually suffered from the effects of those phenomena, as when she was severely cut by pieces of flying glass. Often, however, other people became victims.

Many incidents of this kind can be cited. For example, Joasia's grandfather, Marian Tomecki, was constantly struck in the head by flying shoes. (The unknown force that set in motion the objects around Joasia took a special liking to the family's footwear in addition to their dishes and cutlery.) On another occasion a friend of Joasia's father from work was hit by a large screw while setting up shelves with him in the parlor. When a friend of Joasia's, seventeen-year-old Dorota Sowa, dropped by the Gajewskis in June 1983, a flowerpot that took off from the windowsill nearly hit her in the head. She had to hide behind a cabinet to escape further "bombardment." Several months afterward, when Dorota told us about this incident, she still looked frightened. From then on she visited Joasia far less often. This made little difference, though, because the kinetic effects that first occurred mainly in the Gajewskis' apartment later started to manifest in other places, such as Joasia's school, a movie theater, and a sanatorium, as if they were trailing her.

Lastly, we should mention a mishap involving Dr. Eustachiusz Gadula. During one of his visits to the girl's home, a zooming inkwell splashed his new suit from top to bottom.

The Gajewskis' flat in Czeladz resembles a battlefield. Countless stains and dents on the walls (especially in the hallway, where kinetic effects are most intense), the chipped, badly damaged bathroom door, pieces of glass embedded everywhere, wrecked furniture—all this effectively discourages a renewed attempt to fix up the apartment and make it presentable. We say "renewed attempt" because in 1985 Joasia's father did make such repairs, but his efforts were futile: shortly afterward the hall was totally battered.

This devastation has drained the household budget of the Gajewskis, who are not well off. Ewa's salary as a telephone operator is a meager one; her husband, currently employed in a municipal services enterprise, earns little more. Their combined income is not enough to replace the constantly breaking dishes and other utensils. The family is understandably distraught, particularly the mother, who is a regular bundle of nerves. The continual "earthquakes" in the apartment have a harrowing effect on her. During the first weeks she cried, thinking her daughter was doing this to spite her. When she realized Joasia had no conscious control over what was happening, she gradually accepted the situation. Whenever something flies in the apartment, however, Ewa becomes fearful and anxious.

To make matters worse, there are problems with clothing. Specialists have warned that the youngster must avoid fabrics generating static electricity and they recommend that she wear cotton. It is also hard to find suitable shoes that minimize static charges.

Joasia, it should be noted, wishes to live like her peers despite everything. This requires considerable fortitude and a number of sacrifices on her part.

For example, the girl is very fond of animals, but they appear ill in her presence. It's not that they do not reciprocate the affection she gives them; they simply seem to react more strongly than humans to an overaccumulation of electrical charges in the environment. Joasia's first dog, her beloved poodle, became sick a few weeks after the initial kinetic manifestations, then died. Moreover, the animal exhibited a specific behavior pattern just before the spontaneous movement of objects: it would curl up in a safe place as if sensing imminent danger. The next puppy Joasia brought home also failed to "adjust." The latest dog has adapted to the unusual conditions, and so far everything is fine. What may happen in the future, though, is anyone's guess.

Joasia herself appears quite indifferent to the attempts being made to explain these phenomena. After skimming through books on psychotronics presented to her as a gift (we had the impression she did this more out of courtesy than genuine interest), she buried them deep in a drawer. "Joasia," states Dr. Gadula, "simply does not take note of certain things and considers it a waste of time to investigate them."

When the Gajewskis were still living on Plonow Street, the happenings there occasionally evoked unfriendly reactions to the girl. Some children and even adults called her a "witch" or, less offensively, a "dynamo." No doubt some of the people in the gawking crowds gathered underneath the windows would have volunteered to burn her at the stake if the whole affair had taken place a few centuries earlier.

In the spring of 1983 Joasia was attending primary school in Sosnowiec. As a result of an illness that lasted several weeks and the disruptions that started in April, she fell way behind in her studies. At one point it even seemed likely she would be held back in sixth grade for one more year. There is no telling how things might have turned out if she had not been fortunate to come across excellent teachers who, upon seeing that the child's strange experiences were not delusions, sympathized with her and helped her get through the initial, most difficult period. With this goal in mind, they not only prepared individualized coursework for the youngster but—equally important—also saw to it that a calm atmosphere prevailed at the school and that her fellow pupils stopped taunting her.

We visited Joasia's school many times and always came away with a good impression. We were particularly impressed by the principal, Anna Wudke, and Joasia's young teacher, Janina Ostrowski. Both looked after the girl solicitously and were in constant touch with her parents and doctor. It was no surprise, therefore, that after moving to Czeladz Joasia opted to continue at her old school, which meant a long and tiring commute (over 40 minutes each way).

When we first met Ms. Ostrowski we were most interested in learning how she had managed to create a normal situation in the classroom. Her response: "It wasn't easy, of course, but I realized it wouldn't do any good to ignore the problem, so after Joasia returned to school I decided to devote a special lesson to her. I wanted most of all to eliminate the aura of morbid sensationalism surrounding the whole matter. I wrote a sentence on the blackboard which I used as my central theme: 'Our classmate is just like us, only a little different.' I explained that the things happening around Joasia were odd but had nothing to do with ghosts, and science would discover their cause. My words must have sunk in, for as far as I know, the other kids didn't tease or pick on Joasia anymore. In fact, they even came to identify with her so much that when some foreign journalists visited our school, the students were absolutely thrilled that one of their classmates was the center of public attention."

Sensationalist reports appearing in the press during the early phase of the phenomena claimed that the teenager played various pranks at school, such as knocking the chalk out of a teacher's hand while she was lecturing. This is untrue, just like the story about the priest and the aspergillum. Kinetic effects rarely occurred when Joasia was at school, and the accounts describing them do not seem very credible—with a single exception. One day Joasia came late to class, and because she was afraid of being reprimanded by the teacher she stood by the door, unsure what to do. When she finally grasped the doorknob, a flowerpot simultaneously fell off a shelf for no apparent reason. This happened sometime in the fall of 1983.

Ms. Ostrowski, however, did confirm the girl's telepathic abilities. Joasia, she said, was not always familiar with the material when called upon, particularly if she had to answer a grammar question: "I would then try to help Joasia by formulating the right answer in my mind. This wasn't always intentional on my part. I simply liked the girl very much and unconsciously wanted her to look her best. I observed that immediately afterward, Joasia would answer the question correctly, which in itself would not be so strange were it not for the fact that her sentences were often very similar in construction and style to those I had mentally formulated. Based on many such experiences, I'm sure this couldn't have been due to coincidence alone."

This observation is confirmed indirectly by an incident that occurred in a math class. Ms. Ostrowski had asked Joasia to solve a problem on the blackboard. At first the girl was unable, then, as though guided by a sudden impulse, quickly wrote down the answer. It was completely wrong and she received a failing grade. A closer analysis of this incident, however, revealed an amazing fact that Ms. Ostrowski did not realize until later. It turned out that while Joasia was struggling with the equation at the blackboard, the teacher was already mentally solving the *next* problem, which she intended to dictate. The solution to it was exactly the same as the one her pupil had written on the blackboard.

Joasia admitted in a subsequent conversation with us that at the critical moment she was not even thinking about solving the equation. She had just wanted to satisfy the math teacher, whom she was afraid of. Because she knew the teacher had the answer, she concentrated on her and something "prompted" her what to write.

For the sake of completeness, we must add that in experiments improvised during school lessons (Joasia's classmates asked her to demonstrate what she could do), unusual physical effects occurred at least twice. In the first instance the girl brought her hand to within a few centimeters of a battery and put out a light bulb connected to it. In the second, while passing her hand along a laboratory flask, she caused a stream of potassium permanganate to move perceptibly in the water (a trick nobody else was able to pull off). Without knowing the conditions under which these experiments were performed, it is hard to judge their credibility; however, considering that this account comes from a teacher, they seem worth mentioning.

But the almost identical experiments we conducted with Joasia in front of a camera several months later ended in failure.

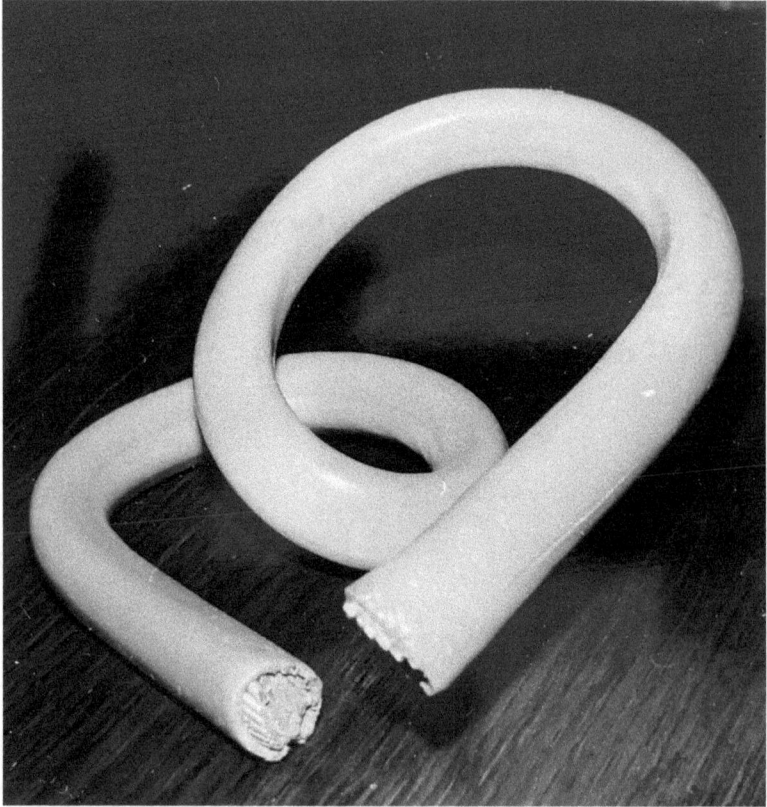

A massive high-tension cable bent by Joasia.

Chapter 4
FIRST COMPREHENSIVE STUDIES

In May 1984, Joasia Gajewski met Dr. Eustachiusz Gadula, who at that time was head of the paraplegic ward at the Miners Medical and Vocational Rehabilitation Center No. 1 in Tarnowskie Gory. In his fifties, this physician and surgeon, who specialized in rehabilitation, is known for his receptiveness toward new developments and trends in medicine, not excluding certain types of so-called alternative therapy. Dr. Gadula is one of the pioneers of acupuncture in Poland, and he has also begun to collaborate with bioenergy therapists (although not without reservations, which he has expressed in many public discussions and speeches). As he has stated—and he has not changed his opinion to date—this approach was dictated to him by one of the cardinal deontological tenets of the medical profession: *"primum non nocere"* (first do no harm). Dr. Gadula simply recognized that if bioenergy therapy can prove helpful in treating certain illnesses, particularly those of psychosomatic origin, there is no reason to reject such assistance.

Participating regularly in symposia organized by psychotronic societies, clubs, and organizations, and following the foreign literature in this field, Dr. Gadula decided to verify personally whether and to what extent it would be possible to study the phenomenon of thirteen-year-old Joasia Gajewski by means of current scientific methods and the latest technology. This endeavor was facilitated by the fact that he quickly won the confidence of the child, who was very distrustful because of the frequent unpleasant experiences she had had with skeptics who treated her like a hoaxer.

His very first visits to the Gajewskis' home convinced Dr. Gadula that the phenomena occurring there were real. Over a relatively brief period, he observed, among other things, amazing acoustical effects in Joasia's presence. Concentrated at first around the girl, they would gradually expand to fill the entire apartment. They were similar to high-voltage discharges; some resembled the scratching of claws or clicking. The doctor captured these sounds on tape. When he played them back shortly afterward for a friend of his, a PhD in physics, the friend said: "Listen, I believe you, but you realize it doesn't prove anything. Such sounds are easy to produce."

"Right," replied Dr. Gadula, "then let's try to study the child under laboratory conditions, which will rule out the possibility of a hoax regardless of the results."

Organizing a scientific team to analyze the phenomenon was no small task, and before it took final shape several weeks had passed. Some specialists in the field did not take the doctor's proposal seriously, while others dropped out because Joasia would not work with them. We should point out that the girl's obstinacy in this kind of situation is such an essential element of her mental makeup that it often precluded experiments from taking place. For this very reason, one of the psychiatrists was removed from the research group: his way of conducting interviews made Joasia "freeze up," whereupon she stubbornly refused to answer any questions.

One more difficulty was that the research had to be organized and financed by those directly involved, as scientific centers in Poland do not provide for the study of parapsychological phenomena in their programs and thus no funds are available for studying them. Thanks to the personal contacts of Dr. Gadula and his colleagues these obstacles were at last overcome, and metallographic and crystallographic analyses of objects twisted in a paranormal manner by Joasia were incorporated in the program of a special institute.

The research project was divided into four sections. The findings obtained in each one would be evaluated jointly. Dr. Gadula directed the medical studies and also served as team chairman. The biophysics research was handled by Dr. Andrzej Franek from the Institute of Biophysics at the Silesian Academy of Medicine and the parapsychology research by Dr. Miroslaw Harciarek from the Institute of Psychology at the University of Silesia. Finally, the metallography studies were supervised by Dr. Klara Cieslak, director of the Institute of Metallography and Welding Technology at the Silesian School of Engineering in Gliwice.

The team worked for several months. The outcome of the project, a report compiled by Dr. Eustachiusz Gadula on October 27, 1983, was submitted to the Ministry of Health and Social Welfare.

Here briefly are its most significant findings. First of all, it should be emphasized that the numerous experiments conducted with Joasia Gajewski have proved *beyond all doubt* that the phenomenon connected with her is real. This was borne out not only by the metal samples she had bent without using physical force at the Institute of Metallography and Welding Technology, and thus under fully controlled conditions (some of these experiments were taped), but above all by the repeated direct observations of researchers who witnessed the paranormal movement of various objects. This definitely banished any doubt concerning the reality of the phenomenon itself. What its mechanisms and causes may be, however, remains an open question.

July 5, 1983, proved to be a landmark date in this regard. Joasia was staying then at the Miners Center for Medical and Vocational Rehabilitation in Repty, where she underwent a series of medical tests and biophysical experiments. It was deemed necessary to isolate the girl from her home environment, which was not conducive to objective observations, and to create a situation in which kinetic phenomena might be induced artificially by irradiating her room with ultraviolet rays.

The test was a complete success.

Let's hear now from the most authoritative observer, Dr. Andrzej Franek from the Institute of Biophysics at the Silesian Academy of Medicine in Zabrze-Rokotnica. We reproduce his statement from a tape recording made on December 15, 1983, when he agreed to give an interview in our presence to a Japanese crew from Fuji Television. We cite here only the salient parts of the interview.

Q. What was the first step in your research?

A. In the initial phase we tried to collect as much information as possible on the phenomenon. We had to rely on the reports of eyewitnesses, some of whom were individuals outside the family. We also read the available literature on the subject. Then we performed preliminary experiments, which, assuming that the phenomenon was real, might yield interesting results of a biophysical nature.

I'd like to draw your attention at this point to a certain methodological problem. Because the phenomenon was unknown to science, it did not fit within the framework of research programs. The kinetic effects occurred with an indeterminable frequency and usually frightened the person observing them. Emotions, as we know, are not conducive to precise reporting. All this shows the magnitude of the difficulties facing us.

[...]

In the final phase–May and June 1983–we tried to determine the child's effect on various fields: gravitational, magnetic, electrostatic, electrical, and electromagnetic. We also observed Joasia bending various objects in a paranormal manner [...] During this period we also attempted to generate kinetic phenomena artificially through the action of certain electromagnetic fields and ionized air. This was essential, inasmuch as these effects were not controlled by the child and they occurred unexpectedly both for her and those around her. We wanted to see if these effects could be produced at will.

Q. Did you succeed?

A. Yes, and we have no doubt that spontaneous movement of objects is a reality. We saw it with our own eyes.

Q. What was it you saw?

A. During Joasia Gajewski's several stays at the hospital, I twice witnessed the paranormal movement of objects. The first occurrence was on July 5, 1983. It happened thirty minutes or so after we began trying to induce the phenomenon by irradiating the room with ultraviolet rays. We heard very curious acoustical effects, which most resembled high-voltage discharges. In Joasia's case, however, they are quite distinctive. There was also a sound similar to the scratching of claws or clicking.

Those effects preceded the spontaneous movement of objects. The first of these was a large, heavy radio-cassette recorder we had wedged in for safety's sake between an armchair and a couch. The recorder was "tossed" into the middle of the room. Next we observed the microphone from a stereo system move several feet. A flashlight lying nearby went into motion and, after traveling a foot or so, struck Dr. Gadula's arm. Then a ping pong ball left in the study after a previous experiment flew about six feet and hit my shoulder. A short time later a canvas shoe resting in a far corner of the room rose from the floor, sailed about ten feet, and struck me in the chest. A rolled-up blanket on the couch glided toward Dr. Gadula and covered him.

It was also interesting to observe the organic changes accompanying all those effects. I noticed that my hair was standing on end and felt a distinct shiver go all the way down my spine to my feet. It seemed as if the air had become highly electrified.

That same evening, we witnessed the movement of an armchair in which Joasia was sitting. Although she had no possibility of affecting the chair (she was sitting with crossed legs and got up when we told her to, which ruled out any trickery on her part), it turned at a sharp angle and rotated rapidly. The magnitude of the forces operating at that moment is evident from the fact that two or three adults could not hold the chair down [Dr. Gadula claims there were four persons: he, Dr. Franek, and two nurses.]

Q. How strong could those forces have been?

A. We don't have data that would allow us to give a precise answer, but we estimate they are quite powerful.

Q. Did you repeat those experiments later on? I mean the attempts to induce the phenomenon by artificial means.

A. Certainly. We made several other attempts, generally with positive results. I'd like to stress, however, that we did not want to abuse this method out of consideration for Joasia, who feels ill and complains of severe headaches after her room is irradiated with ultraviolet rays. The matter thus has a serious ethical aspect. One mustn't lose sight of that.

Q. Has the team managed to film the spontaneous movement of objects?

A. Not yet. There are technical obstacles. We would need in particular an apparatus sensitive to infrared. But since several of us observed those effects numerous times, it's safe to assume they can be objectively recorded on film.

Q. What are the general findings of your biophysics research?

A. It's still too early for specifics. All the research findings must be evaluated jointly after the project is completed. I can only say that at the present time we see certain interesting connections between two discrete types of fields, electromagnetic and electrostatic, and that such connections don't occur in a person with normal reactions. We wish to present our ideas on this subject in scientific journals.

Q. Does that mean you are close to solving the mystery?

A. Studies of psychokinetic phenomena are being conducted in many laboratories throughout the world. Everyone expects a straightforward explanation, and that's the thorniest problem [...] I would suggest that we place the emphasis on something else. Ludwik Hershfeld, the discoverer of blood groups and one of the "fathers" of Polish immunology, once told his students that if you are dealing with a very difficult scientific problem, the most important thing is to formulate the question properly. Only then can you proceed step by step to the answer. We would be delighted, after the several months' work we've done, if we could formulate the right question.

Q. Do you believe it will be possible to explain this phenomenon on the basis of the known laws of physics?

A. The problem is more philosophical than physical in nature. I believe that just as Einstein and his colleagues expected that a "link" would be found between all potential fields, perhaps the phenomena we are studying will lead to the discovery of new, interesting laws of physics. [End of recording]

Dr. Franek's statement can be substantiated with additional information. During the biophysics studies and experiments conducted with Joasia, she affected magnetic needles, closed circuits, and radio waves of various frequencies. Other experiments involved attempts to discharge (by touch) electroscopes and condensers. Most of these experiments failed, which means only that they did not enable the researchers to detect any discrete, verifiable physical phenomena (although there were some amazing results here too, such as Joasia's discharging an electroscope).

Dr. Franek's conclusion regarding the existence, in the girl's case, of "interesting connections between electromagnetic and electrostatic fields," which do not occur in a person with normal reactions, represents the synthesis of months of diligent research. The honesty and candor with which the Silesian biophysicist reported his findings cannot be emphasized enough. For it is no secret that Dr. Franek, when accepting Dr. Gadula's offer to join the scientific team and direct the biophysics section, did not conceal his skepticism toward the existence of the phenomenon (as he admitted later in a conversation with us, he felt sure that trickery was involved). This caused some difficulties, since Joasia, as if sensing Dr. Franek's reservations, would "freeze up" mentally during the experiments. Consequently, the two of them did not work very well together at first. But the encouraging results of certain experiments designed by Dr. Franek, and especially his direct observations of phenomena that he as a physicist had every right to doubt, enabled him to break through this impasse and arrive at conclusions far removed from hidebound, inside-the-box thinking.

One of the most eminent figures in Polish medicine today, Professor Julian Aleksandrowicz, said in a conversation with us in December 1985 that there is a fundamental difference between the scientist and the scholar. In the professor's opinion, only someone who has the courage to pursue and uphold the truth regardless of his colleagues' reactions, the etiquette of his profession, and conventional wisdom deserves to be called a scholar.

The psychological studies performed on Joasia were directed by Dr. Miroslaw Harciarek from the Institute of Psychology at the University of Silesia. We conducted an extensive interview with Dr. Harciarek (see "Appendix 1. Hypotheses") but present here just an excerpt of his important findings. He stated that his aim "was to gather preliminary data which might be of some value in compiling Joasia Gajewski's psychological portrait. While the information we obtained didn't contribute any new insights into psychokinesis, it served as a starting point for more concrete hypotheses and allowed us to compare the girl's test results with those of other children in her age group."

Q. Can you briefly summarize your findings?

A. As far as the standard psychological tests are concerned, no significant deviations from the norm were found. Therefore, our personality assessment couldn't single out which of Joasia's mental traits is related to psychokinesis. We only managed to formulate general guidelines for subsequent research.

On the other hand, the sensory and lateralization tests all indicated that future studies should be designed in such a way as to help us better understand the functioning of the girl's cerebral hemispheres. This was an important finding, since many earlier researchers on psychic phenomena associated them with the functioning of the hemispheres, particularly the right one.

Here I made use of my own experiments with afterimages. These are visual images that arise from stimulation of the optic system, such as the colored spots one sees after looking at the sun. The connection of afterimages with the functional asymmetry of the cerebral hemispheres is twofold. First, afterimages are conditioned by the activity of the cerebral hemispheres; and second, from what we know about the relation between the eyeballs and the hemispheres, when examining afterimages in the left or right eye we indirectly study the functioning of the individual hemispheres. Using afterimages to explore the workings of the brain also seems relevant because with special techniques we can ascertain the transfer of stimuli between the two hemispheres. This can't be accomplished with other methods.

Q. Did you discover anything peculiar?

A. The results of studies on the afterimages in Joasia's eyes show heightened activity in her right hemisphere. The afterimages it produced were multicolored and clearly differentiated, whereas those in the left one were less differentiated, often fragmentary, momentary, and usually achromatic. I should mention that other people do not exhibit such pronounced asymmetry, that is, such a great discrepancy between the afterimages of the left and right hemispheres.

Q. What do you conclude from this?

A. When I examined the girl's afterimages with a different method, I found that those from the right hemisphere lasted longer, which is typical of normal individuals. At the same time, however, I made a finding that must be considered quite extraordinary: there was an intensive transfer of afterimages from the right to the left hemisphere, but not vice-versa. It was four times greater than normal and contrary to what's expected. This can be interpreted as tension stemming from the joint activity of the hemispheres, with the tension moving from the right to the left hemisphere.

[...]

Another remarkable finding relates to chromatic afterimages. To illustrate what I mean by this term, let's take the following example. When we look at a green circle for thirty seconds and then shift our eyes to a white sheet of paper, we see a red circle on it. This is a chromatic afterimage. The colors that such images have are complementary to the colors of the stimuli producing them, which means that a red stimulus produces a green afterimage, a yellow stimulus–a blue afterimage, and vice versa. But in Joasia Gajewski's case it turns out that only a single form of chromatic afterimage appeared–red, generated by a blue stimulus. Red, green, and yellow stimuli did not produce afterimages. The red afterimages, moreover, were not complementary, for a blue stimulus ought to produce a yellow afterimage. I should note (to cite Goscimierz Geras) that a shift in complementary colors, such as a blue stimulus gaining a red afterimage, occurs in people with a malfunctioning thyroid gland.

Q. The medical studies did not reveal anything wrong with the girl's thyroid.

A. Then the finding becomes even more intriguing, especially if we bear in mind that chromatic afterimages, contrary to orthodox views, are connected not only with the functioning of the eye itself but also with the energy processes occurring in the neurohormonal system and with the activity of the cerebral hemispheres. It's claimed that hormonal substances, by dissolving asymmetrically in both hemispheres, cause a differentiation in their activity, which leads to their functional asymmetry. The asymmetry and energy processes of the hemispheres determine in turn the chromatic afterimages. Consequently, the study of afterimages can be looked upon as investigating the energy processes occurring in the brain.

Q. Do you mean that Joasia's chromatic afterimages may reflect her mental processes?

A. That's exactly what I think. But the matter doesn't end there. Analyses done by Ewa Panek confirmed that the girl had certain hormonal anomalies. The level of dopamine in Joasia's urine turned out to be very low relative to the norm. This finding was very important, for variations in the amount of dopamine in the body are closely associated with mental processes. Researchers studying the biochemistry of the brain had noted long ago a lower level of dopamine in the brain during epileptic seizures, and a higher level in the case of schizophrenic symptoms. Hence the results obtained in Joasia Gajewski's case pointed to a clinical picture of epilepsy.

Q. Does that mean you consider psychic phenomena a form of epilepsy?

A. That I don't know. But it does seem interesting that epilepsy is also related to the functioning of the cerebral hemispheres. Incidentally, some types of epilepsy are treated surgically by cutting the corpus callosum uniting the hemispheres, whose joint activity is so vital for the energy processes in the mind.

Q. Experiments with Joasia Gajewski also included studies on her cognitive processes and language…

A. They likewise indicated a close relationship between the processes in the girl's cerebral hemispheres and the functioning of her nervous system. For example, it turned out that Joasia's verbal associations for noun stimuli denoting objects subjected to psychokinesis can be described as "inhibited." They were usually repetitions, diminutives, or a form of the same word. These associations referred to the phonetic aspect of the given stimulus, not to its content.

Q. Why is that significant?

A. Analysis of the associations shows that words denoting objects subjected to psychokinesis were excluded from the youngster's conscious mind and repressed in her subconscious. The results of our studies can be correlated with the workings of the cerebral hemispheres to the extent that the conscious mind is connected with the functioning of the left hemisphere, and the subconscious mind with the functioning of the right. The semantic field of words that denote objects subjected to psychokinesis, and that are probably in the left hemisphere (which is linked more closely to language and speech), was controlled by the right hemisphere, or the subconscious.

[…]

Q. Did you also consider the whole matter from the viewpoint of psychoanalysis?

A. Of course. After thoroughly acquainting myself with many details pertaining to Joasia and her family, I found a neat correlation between the psychokinetic effects and the family situation. According to this approach, psychokinetic attacks symbolize the girl's need for a closer relationship with her father as well as the difficulties she has in relating to her mother. Thus, psychokinetic phenomena reflect the girl's emotional state.

[End of interview excerpt.]

Dr. Eustachiusz Gadula supervised the medical research on Joasia. In view of its very broad scope and complexity, the assistance of many specialists was required. This is quite understandable, given that the project embraced psychiatry, internal medicine, and neurology, and included a series of special procedures such as electrocardiography, electroencephalography, CT brain scans, thermography, and study of the deep structures of the eye.

In view of the obligation to respect medical confidentiality, we must confine ourselves to presenting just some of the observations and conclusions from all these endeavors. The most significant finding is this: from the medical viewpoint Joasia Gajewski is generally healthy. We say "generally," for surely there is no one who does not have some ailment to complain of. In Joasia's case this was and still is her fairly frequent colds; however, nothing was found that would lead one to assume the presence of distinct anomalies affecting the functioning of the girl's body and her state of health. The strongest evidence for this conclusion comes from the results of the encephalographic examinations, which were within the normal range.

The thermographic studies proved to be quite intriguing. Photographs taken revealed puzzling "thermal spots" in certain areas of the girl's body, especially around the fingers, toes, head, and slightly above the solar plexus. Their cause has not been definitively established, but it is possible they are foci of highly condensed energy accompanied by the elevated temperatures that have been recorded.

Fluctuations in Joasia's temperature likewise pose an enigma. There have been days, for example, when a thermometer placed in her armpit reads 41°C (105.8°F), which is an abnormally high fever, then plummets after a while to 35.8°C (96.44°F), which is below normal. This took place on April 10-11, 1986, when an emergency medical team was summoned to the girl; the doctors, though, could find nothing wrong with her. Professor Lech J. Radwanowski, who witnessed a similar occurrence in May 1983, used a special probe for so-called instantaneous measurement of temperature. Although the thermometer showed a dangerously elevated reading of 43°C (109.6°F), the probe indicated that the girl's body temperature was approximately 37°C (98.6°F), which is normal body temperature.

This observation concerning the lack of correlation between the readings on the thermometer and the probe was confirmed indirectly by Dr. Gadula (who claims that he may be only slightly off when estimating a patient's temperature). He too is convinced that Joasia's body temperature at a critical moment is usually normal or only slightly elevated. This would mean that the youngster herself affects the mercury column in the thermometer in some inexplicable way. Thus far no one has been able to determine just how this happens.

There were still more surprises. For example, during the project the electrostatic charges on Joasia's skin were measured regularly, and they turned out to be very high. This in itself would not be significant, for we live in an environment where we constantly "collect" charges from our surroundings, and before they are discharged (causing the "kicking effect" at autopsies) they can become quite high. The problem in Joasia's case is that they are not dissipated by grounding, i.e., not discharged when she touches metal objects.

A control group underwent similar tests. Their charges proved to be considerably lower or close to zero. The sole exception was a nurse whose charges were higher than Joasia's. After publishing this information in an article, we received a letter from Mr. Grzegorz Zapalski, a staff member of the Nuclear Research Institute in Krakow with whom we had been in contact previously. He expressed skepticism toward the connection between the static charges discovered on Joasia's skin and the kinetic effects around her. Zapalski considers this a secondary effect to which no importance should be attached. He writes: "If the girl wears a nylon sweater, a wool blouse, and rubber or plastic-sole shoes, that will be enough for her to accumulate thirty or forty thousand volts of static electricity and to emit sparks several centimeters [...] This may also apply to the deflection of the magnetic needle of a compass (even through a glass pane) when an electrostatically charged finger comes near it. What is really operating here is coulombic forces, which are responsible for electrostatic attraction and repulsion, and which we have known about for over a hundred years."

We accept this line of reasoning, but with one caveat. As we mentioned before, shortly after the initial experiments, which gave rise to suspicion that excessively high electrostatic charges were accumulating on Joasia's skin, special care was taken that she not wear any clothes made of nylon, wool, or other easily electrified materials (similar precautions were taken in regard to her shoes as well). Nevertheless, the charges measured later on were scarcely different from the earlier ones and (we must re-emphasize) could not be "grounded." Or is it possible—and this is only our conjecture—that in Joasia's case they are generated more quickly than they are discharged through "grounding?"

But this matter seems to belong more to physics than to medicine. What Dr. Gadula terms "very odd muscular activity," however, should be considered a strictly medical phenomenon. It manifests (while the girl is asleep or resting in a recumbent position) in periodic strong, frequent muscular twitching or rather contractions, which induce peculiar microvibrations. This occurs most often when Joasia has a headache or complains of feeling unwell. At times her atypical muscular activity becomes so intense that it produces kinetic effects.

That is exactly what happened one night during the teenager's stay at the rehabilitation center in Repty. The nurses on duty heard odd noises coming from the office where she was sleeping (she had been placed there so as not to disturb the patients). Alerted, they immediately summoned the head of the paraplegic ward, Dr. Gadula. A moment later these three fully aware adults witnessed a phenomenon that violated every law of physics. As a result of the increasing vibrations and shaking, the couch where Joasia was sitting with her mother and the doctor suddenly rose several inches off the floor, then came back down with a thud.

During the teenager's several stays at the hospital in Repty other amazing phenomena occurred. Too many people saw them for these observations to be dismissed solely as optical illusions. One such incident merits special attention.

In the autumn of 1985 Joasia began complaining of pain in the abdominal area. A medical examination revealed chronic appendicitis; what's more, it turned out that the appendix itself was wrongly positioned. Her condition being serious, the decision was made to operate.

Dr. Gadula, who was in charge of the girl's treatment, decided to perform the operation himself after obtaining permission from his superiors (which was necessary because the paraplegic ward did not as a rule accept patients with acute illnesses, i.e., those requiring surgery). Dr. Gadula, of course, knew Joasia best; he had to be present in the event of any non-medical "surprises."

"Imagine," he said half-facetiously in a conversation with us, "what would have happened if the surgeon's instruments began to 'slip away' during the procedure? It may sound funny, but I couldn't forget for a second that I'd seen all sorts of kinetic effects, which would occur at the most unexpected moments. So we had to be extra-careful in this instance."

Because the spontaneous movement of objects often took place while the girl slept, Dr. Gadula opted for local instead of general anesthesia.

He recalls: "Joasia came through the operation splendidly. Only seven hours later she was in the corridor talking, joking, and laughing with the other patients. Just then, I was told, something happened—the very thing I had most dreaded while performing the appendectomy. It occurred the day after the operation. A traction brace—a rehabilitation device for propping up the leg, a kind of hook made of thick wire—came streaking right through the open door of her room. The brace flew around in the strangest way: it bounced off the door of the room opposite Joasia's, then, according to observers, headed with an undulating movement in a totally different direction."

We found out later that an elderly woman patient who had witnessed this incident was unable to regain her senses for some time. To her, what she had seen was irrefutable proof of sorcery.

"I should mention another significant fact," said Dr. Gadula, "the postoperative sutures on the girl's body opened up immediately, as if some kind of internal force had torn them apart. [The doctor assured us that the sutures were sewn with the utmost care.] The wound healed only after we put in new sutures—this time without any complications."

When children play hide-and-seek, they help the searcher with the traditional "you're cold, warm, hot." Around Joasia Gajewski of Sosnowiec, it is always hot. But Dr. Gadula's team pursued its research with cool scientific detachment, without which any valid, credible results are difficult to imagine.

When considered in their entirety, the team's results fall short in a number of areas, at least for the purposes of our account. One such area is the findings of the metallographic studies conducted at the Institute of Metallography and Welding Technology in Gliwice under the supervision of Dr. Klara Cieslak. This is regrettable, for in certain respects these studies had been the most promising. Among the many phenomena associated with the Sosnowiec teenager, the bending of flatware and various metal items without the application of physical force was the most tangible, in that it left behind concrete evidence of paranormal action and represented the sole example of a consciously directed phenomenon and its concomitant effects. Compared with objects hurtling through the air at a tremendous velocity and wreaking havoc all around, the bending of a teaspoon by rubbing it with two fingers may seem trivial indeed. We advise those who hold this view to try doing it themselves.

During our many visits to Sosnowiec we often observed Joasia bending various kinds of objects in a paranormal manner. We received several of these items as souvenirs. One is a thick communications cable twisted into a lovely bow. There are also spoons twisted into elaborate shapes more reminiscent of metalworking than of psychotronic experiments. But a metalworker subjects his materials to high temperatures, whereas Joasia merely uses two fingers of her hand.

This experiment, in all honesty, does not always succeed. For instance, Joasia was unable for a long time to bend tableware in the presence of a camera. It seemed as though filming disconcerted her and threw off her concentration. This mental block was eventually overcome, which does not mean of course that she can always perform the task assigned to her.

In the presence of a large group of people, many of whom expect immediate results or who are genuinely skeptical of them, the metal-bending occurs more slowly and sometimes ends in failure. We say "sometimes," for it is undeniable that she has managed to bend numerous metal objects even under such adverse psychological conditions. She was particularly successful in experiments at the Institute of Metallography and Welding Technology, as well as in the test she underwent in 1984 at the Institute of Physics at Jagiellonian University in Krakow (see the chapter "No Possibility of a Hoax").

In this context, it would be interesting to determine to what extent a researcher's attitude toward observed phenomena affects Joasia's mental blocks. Here we can cite the following example. When Dr. Gadula's team started its work, one of the scientists, who was consulted on the methodology of the proposed experiments, expressed great skepticism that the youngster would be able to bend utensils in the described manner. He would say bluntly: "I'll believe it when I see it."

The skeptic was therefore invited to participate in the experiment. When Joasia bent a spoon, the professor revised his previous criterion of belief and disbelief and declared he would only accept the phenomenon if the girl bent not one spoon but ten right before his eyes. In the unlikely event she had managed to pull this off, the observer would have demanded that she bend a hundred items in his presence.

Another time, during one of our visits to Czeladz, we had the following experience. We asked Joasia, in the presence of two scientists, to bend a spoon belonging to us. The girl, who seemed to be a little weary of these "games," wondered if the spoon would be part of the studies or if we wanted it as a "souvenir." We asked her what difference it made. She replied that of course it made a difference, because she was fed up with bending things for scientific purposes, but she liked us, and if we wanted a bent spoon as a souvenir that was a different matter. Thereupon she bent the spoon in a couple of minutes before everyone's eyes.

What may appear at first to be a teenage girl's whims will become more understandable if one considers that for the purposes of studies conducted since June 1983 at the Institute of Metallography and Welding Technology, Joasia Gajewski bent several dozen spoons, forks, knives, bars, cables, and similar metal items. Science, which values statistics and the law of big numbers more highly than many other disciplines, constantly called for more data, and like it or not the demand had to be met. In spite of the pressure, Joasia grew fond of Professor Cieslak, and they are still close. Nonetheless, after several years of painstaking metallographic research the findings remain puzzling.

We first spoke with Professor Cieslak in December 1983 during our stay at the Gliwice School of Engineering. We marveled at row upon row of metal objects and cutlery bent by Joasia. They had been (or were to be) carefully numbered and described as the subject of detailed metallographic research, which was expected to wrap up in the autumn of 1984.

According to information we received, and which we discussed with others, including Drs. Elzbieta and Wojciech Ozgowicz, both staff members of the Institute, it turned out that the comprehensive studies were based on a comparison of spoons bent by Joasia with those bent by other people using physical force. The studies involved the deep structure of matter—beginning with an analysis of the metallographic level, proceeding to the crystalline structures, and ending with the atomic bonds. We learned what while highly sensitive equipment, including electron and X-ray microscopes, would be required to achieve full, clear-cut results, the findings obtained up to that point seemed to indicate basic differences in the structure of metal samples bent in a conventional manner (i.e., through physical force) and those bent by the girl in a paranormal manner. In the latter instance, there was supposedly not only a deformation of the atomic bonds but also specific changes in the crystalline structures.

Toward the end of 1985 we learned from one of the staff members conducting experiments with Joasia Gajewski by a new, interdisciplinary team under the auspices of the Institute for Mother and Child (see the chapter "No Possibility of a Hoax") that the metallographic studies were essentially completed, and that their results were negative in this respect: the metal samples bent by Joasia did not show any differences compared with the control samples bent by other persons using physical force. Mr. and Mrs. Gajewski received the same results.

Confused by this contrary information, in late December 1985 we sent a letter to Professor Ciesak, asking for clarification of the final results. For we believed that even if the findings in this area were disappointing, there was no reason to conceal the fact, especially as they in themselves did not prove anything. That Joasia bends metal objects in a paranormal manner is an established fact, and in this situation one can speak most of a failure to find detectable (by a single science, metallography) elements that would make it possible to explain the mechanism and effects of the phenomenon.

Having received no reply to our letter, on the day before our next visit to Czeladz on March 13, 1986, we phoned Dr. Cieslak to request an interview. This proved to be impossible. We were informed that first of all, it was difficult to speak of final results because a student who was writing his master's thesis on the experiment had been drafted into the army and taken all the material with him, and second, it could not be ruled out that the metal samples used in previous experiments had been poorly chosen since nobody had taken into account the impurities arising during the manufacturing of the various spoons, which would create additional deformation and different dense structures, and thus might affect the results.

Unfortunately, we were unable to otherwise discover the reasons for the discrepancy between the information we received in December 1983 (distinct differences and changes in the crystalline structure of metal) and the conclusions presented to us two and a half years later.

Afterward we made one more attempt to solicit an opinion on this matter. We consulted Zygmunt Hasia, an eminent scientist and the director of the Institute of Commercial Materials and Metal Technology at the Lodz School of Engineering. Professor Hasia, as we learned from the daily press, was performing a similar experiment (i.e., spoon-bending without the use of physical force) with nine-year-old Agnieszka Stopczyk of Lodz. His statement for the newspaper *Express Ilustrowany* (no. 57/85) included the following remarks:

"On the basis of what I have seen, as well as other reports, it can be said this is not a supernatural phenomenon [...] One can try to interpret it even without conducting experiments and studies, although they are necessary. We know the mechanism whereby the metal of spoons is deformed. Deformation results from so-called slippage and twinning. No one questions anymore the existence of a biofield, which under favorable conditions may cause dislocations responsible for slippage in materials [...] One can hypothesize that deformation results from resonance by vibrations in the biofield, and this occurs if their frequency is equal or close to the vibrations in the atomic network of the metal [...] I believe this problem should be tackled not only to satisfy our curiosity but also to expand scientific horizons."

Wishing to expand scientific horizons, we got in touch with Professor Hasia and arranged a mutually convenient time to meet. Unfortunately, in spite of our careful preparation for this meeting, the Lodz scientist did not show up and never explained why he dropped the idea of collaborating with us. Thus, the story of Joasia Gajewski's metallographic "adventures" has reached a dead end.

In conclusion, we think it worthwhile to provide some additional information. According to data provided by the president of the Japanese Society for the Study of Extrasensory Perception, Dr. Toshiya Nakaoka (who visited Warsaw in 1974), laboratory metallographic studies of flatware bent in a paranormal manner by Japanese sensitives, particularly by the most famous of them, Jun Sekiguchi, yielded extremely interesting results. For it turned out that the arrangement of the grain of the metal on the place where an object had been deformed by this method was totally different than when a spoon was bent through the application of physical force. In the former instance the structure of the grain purportedly exhibited features of parallelism, whereas in the latter it was disturbed: the grain appeared to be cracked or was arranged in a wavelike pattern. In studies of steel spoons, the researchers also noted the so-called ridge effect, which they claim cannot be produced by bending metal through the action of a definite mechanical force. The experts at the metallography lab in Chi-ba-chi concluded: "The spoons were bent by means of some unknown force." In short, we were back where we began.

The comprehensive studies conducted from May to October 1983 by the team supervised by Dr. Eustachiusz Gadula were summarized in a lengthy letter sent on October 27 of that year to the Ministry of Health and Social Welfare.

Tarnowskie Gory
October 27, 1983
The Ministry of Health and Social Welfare
Warsaw

I would like to request that consideration be given to establishing a departmental program of comprehensive studies on the phenomenon of Joasia Gajewski of Sosnowiec.

In April 1983, the media in Silesia and then throughout Poland reported that in Sosnowiec a thirteen-year-old girl named Joanna Gajewski had begun exhibiting paranormal abilities, manifested in the odd behavior of objects in her immediate vicinity. According to accounts given by Joasia, her parents and other relatives, and neighbors, on April 4 of this year objects of every kind in the girl's vicinity started flying about spontaneously. Within several days the apartment in which she and her parents lived became badly damaged. Most of the glass articles were shattered, including many of the panes in the windows and in various pieces of furniture, as well as a number of household utensils. The furniture and walls sustained damage. The frightened parents sought help from the local authorities and the public health service. At the height of this telekinetic activity the girl was observed to be in poor condition, with an elevated body temperature, headaches, and marked irritability.

Initial attempts to obtain assistance proved unsuccessful. Everywhere the Gajewskis met with disbelief or outright derision. The doctors whom they repeatedly sent for could not find anything seriously wrong with the child's health, and many of them were inclined to perceive symptoms of collective hysteria in the family's behavior. It was not until the media interceded with the local authorities that the mayor of Sosnowiec ordered officials of the Civil Militia to observe these phenomena and draw up a formal report.

Because the first observers of the above phenomena

47

[...], who had familiarity with the problem, conjectured that they might be caused by the particularly unfavorable location of the apartment with respect to ground radiation and the girl's own paranormal abilities, the Gajewskis received a new apartment several weeks later. Despite the change of residence, however, the previously observed phenomena continued to occur intermittently.

Both Joasia and her parents were in a state of extreme nervous exhaustion attributable to a number of factors:
a. the parents' anxiety about their child's health;
b. fear caused by the phenomena, which were not only incomprehensible but dangerous to the family;
c. considerable financial losses, with little chance that they would be reimbursed by the PZU [Polish National Insurance];
d. the nasty, sometimes vicious reactions of neighbors and others in the community.

At the beginning of May I was approached with respect to this matter and asked if I, as a person engaged in alternative therapies and interested in paranormal phenomena, would like to study the girl. After thinking it over for several days and gaining the cooperation of the Institute of Biophysics at the Silesian Academy of Medicine and the Institute of Psychology at the University of Silesia, I agreed.

We divided the studies into three sections:
1. Medical (interviews, physical examinations, numerous consultations, and necessary non-invasive instrumental studies);
2. Psychological (evaluation of the mental state of the girl and her parents, and attempts to improve it);
3. Biophysical (a series of biophysical experiments that would help clarify the nature of the observed phenomena). [...]

Several weeks later the girl tried successfully to bend objects, mainly flatware, in a paranormal manner. She was often able to perform this feat at will. Having discovered her new ability, we contacted the Institute of

Metallography at the Gliwice School of Engineering, which planned extensive research, principally metallographic, on the objects affected by the girl.

The studies conducted by the medical section found no severe pathology and dispelled fears of a serious danger to the subject's life and health.

The psychological studies revealed that Joasia and especially her mother had a heightened level of nervous excitability, but no pronounced psychopathological traits. During this period, psychological treatment by members of the research team improved the mother's condition slightly and the girl's considerably. Joasia, who in the early spring had to face the possibility of being held back for another year, graduated to seventh grade without much difficulty at the end of the year.

After the director of the Miners Medical and Vocational Rehabilitation Center in Tarnowskie Gory, Dr. Boguslaw Matin, gave his consent, the girl and her mother stayed at our institution twice for observation. Their first stay was in mid-May 1983. During the three days of preliminary observation Joasia Gajewski underwent several examinations, had an EEG test, and was the subject of biophysical experiments. During this time she bent six teaspoons in the presence of members of the research team. A seventh spoon broke while she was attempting to bend it; the resulting sound was recorded on tape.

In the course of the girl's three-week stay at the rehabilitation center in July, regular observation was supplemented with CT scans, thermographic studies, and examinations and photographs of her eyes. We often heard and taped strange acoustical effects, which usually preceded the telekinetic phenomena.

On three occasions we observed undoubtedly paranormal movement of objects in the consulting room where Joasia and her mother were lodged while at the center. Most of the telekinetic phenomena occurred in the dark or in dim light. Only once during the girl's stay at our institution did two members of the team manage

49

to see an object in flight. I should mention that these phenomena were witnessed not only by members of the research group but also by nurses on duty in our ward and two physicians from other wards.

I last observed telekinetic phenomena in the Gajews-kis' apartment three weeks ago. This time they occurred in bright electric light. Although the lighting enabled me to monitor the girl closely, not once was I able to perceive an object in flight–the phenomenon was over in an instant. That evening I had occasion to observe the paranormal change in position of a dozen or so objects, including sharp metal ones. [...]

Telekinetic phenomena still occur at the Gajewski residence, causing further damage to their possessions and the apartment itself. Repeated attempts to obtain compensation from the PZU have been unavailing, because there are no legal grounds for such payment: Polish law does not provide for compensation of losses resulting from the operation of paranormal forces. [...] The family is justifiably bitter about this, especially as there is no sign that these phenomena will end anytime soon.

As a result of information presented in the mass media and in a report of the Polish Biocenotic Society given at the International Psychotronic Congress in Bratislava, the media both here and abroad have been exerting heavy pressure for months to sensationalize the Joasia Gajewski story. Behind this pressure is the desire of certain interested parties to line their pockets. [...] Three months ago, for example, Joasia's parents were approached by representatives of two foreign Polish-owned companies who proposed that their daughter go on a world tour for money. Several television crews in the West are impatiently waiting for permission to start filming.

As soon as our team undertook this project, we obtained the consent of Joasia's parents to turn down media requests for interviews and documentaries until we completed the preliminary studies and issued a statement through the Polish Press Agency. After much con-

sideration, however, we concluded that such a statement would do little to aid the Gajewski family (at least
in their efforts to obtain compensation from the PZU),
and that once it came out both the family and the researchers would be besieged by the media again.

We see a need for further studies on the girl by means
of special equipment, and for incontrovertible documentation of the telekinetic phenomena. [...] Above all,
the Gajewski family must be allowed to live a normal
life. Inasmuch as our team and the administration of
the rehabilitation center in Repty cannot meet all these
needs, we propose that the Ministry of Health consider
establishing a departmental program to explore the
problem.

We have good reason to believe that if the Ministry
rejects this conclusion, the girl's parents will agree to
collaborate on a regular basis with a foreign contractor.
This would represent an undeniable loss for both Polish
medicine and the entire Polish scientific community.

[Signed] Dr. Eustachiusz Gadula, head of the paraplegic
ward at the Miners Medical and Vocational Rehabilitation Center No. I in Repty

The ultimate fate of this proposal will be discussed in a subsequent chapter. First, however, we wish to recount two events
that happened at the end of 1983 and the beginning of 1984, and
whose importance for understanding the Gajewski phenomenon
cannot be overestimated.

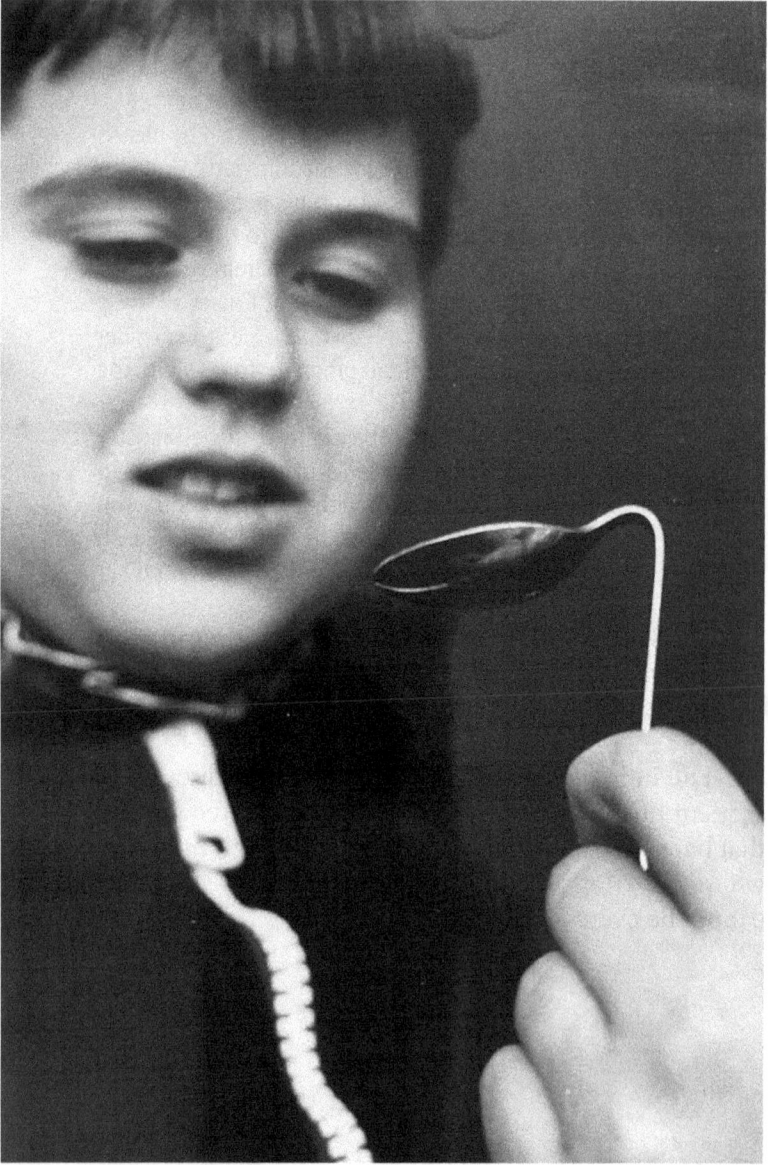

Joasia with a spoon bent psychokinetically.

Chapter 5
THE COLD EYE OF THE CAMERA

On December 12, 1983, a crew from the biggest Japanese TV channel, Fuji Television, arrived in Poland to shoot a special program on Joasia Gajewski's psychokinetic abilities and other remarkable psychic phenomena in Poland. This project was part of a new weekly series on Fuji that featured paranormal phenomena from all over the world and sought to give a scientific explanation for them. The crew was headed by Toshio Uruta, the channel's director of popular science programming.

The arrival of the Japanese was preceded by drawn-out negotiations. For as Dr. Gadula mentioned in his report, under the arrangement between the team conducting research with Joasia Gajewski and her parents, contacts with journalists in the form of interviews, conversations, news stories, etc. were suspended until the Ministry of Health and Social Welfare reached a decision on whether further steps were needed with respect to the scientific investigation of the phenomenon. During this period we were the only reporters collaborating with Dr. Gadula and his team, following developments as they occurred while fully respecting—in the interest of the ongoing research and the youngster herself—the embargo on publication.

The consent given by the research team and Joasia's parents to collaborate with the Japanese crew signaled a departure from the previous general principle to maintain an information blockade. Two factors were decisive here. First, the Fuji Television crew—in contrast to many others—had a solid professional background as far as journalistic familiarity with the topic was concerned (its members had already produced documentaries about various borderland phenomena and gone on frequent trips from Mexico to the Philippines). This ensured a serious, dispassionate approach to the subject. But the second argument carried the most weight. Contact with the Fuji reporters, apart from an exchange of experience and information (their earlier programs on diverse parapsychological phenomena), afforded a unique opportunity to shoot a documentary using the crew's equipment, something the Silesian research team could only dream about. Of particular interest were the ultramodern camera and video recorder, which the visitors agreed to install for a while in the Gajewskis' apartment in the hope that continuous monitoring would make it possible to register kinetic effects on a cassette. This was a really tempting offer, especially when combined with the promise by the Japanese to copy the cassette and send it to the Polish researchers if the recording proved successful.

Apart from Toshio Uruta, the other crew members were Takashi Tachibana, a well- known writer in Japan and author of many widely read books and TV documentaries; Yohji Itagaki, production director; Yoshihiro Itoh, cameraman; and Yoichi Hirai, sound engineer. All of them, we came to see, were professionals of the highest caliber. Unfortunately, however, the results of their work turned out to be far less useful than we had expected.

The reason for this was that Joasia happened to be indisposed during the filmmakers' week-long stay in Poland. Even before their arrival she had complained of various aches and pains (the girl had undergone an operation at the hospital in Repty the previous month). Above all she found it extremely hard to concentrate, so most of the experiments performed in front of the camera failed to come off. This was especially upsetting because some of the earlier ones had been successful. Worse still, during the few times Joasia sat in front of the camera, she was unable to bend spoons, but after the filming stopped she managed to do it easily before the eyes of the whole crew and others present.

The Japanese guests felt terribly disappointed. Recognizing that experiments in front of the camera, particularly those with children, often fail (spoon-bending experiments with a selected group of girls and boys were also being filmed in Japan), they were piqued not so much by the unsatisfactory outcome as by Joasia's basic lack of concentration. The Japanese believed, not without good reason, that if the teenager made a determined effort she could overcome her difficulties. Moreover, they said, it might be possible for the girl to control at least to some degree the psychokinetic phenomena around her.

Regrettably, we must admit that Joasia's personality is such that it is exceedingly hard, if not downright impossible, to expect her to be like her compliant peers in the Far East. This is particularly true in regard to her concentration problem, which is quite apparent at school. Another complicating factor is the mother's extremely high-strung temperament.

The Japanese guests did not skimp on their film. Besides the material shot in the apartment, they interviewed many eyewitnesses of the psychokinetic phenomena. They also visited the Institute of Biophysics at the Academy of Medicine in Zabrze-Rokotnica and the Documentation Center at the Gliwice School of Engineering, where they spent six hours watching VCR tapes of the metallographic, medical, and biophysical experiments conducted with Joasia.

In regard to the experiments carried out during the film crew's visit to Silesia, several things are worth noting. Let's begin with the most important: the attempt to record kinetic phenomena on VCR tape. It succeeded in only a single instance. But this was a partial success, for we had failed to take one crucial factor into account: the tremendous velocity of spontaneously moving objects. This velocity far exceeds that of a similar object thrown by hand. We had occasion to see this for ourselves on December 13, 1983, or rather on the following day.

December 13, which fell on a Tuesday, was spent almost entirely in shooting film in the Czeladz apartment, including the first spoon-bending trials improvised in front of the camera, a partially successful attempt to move ping pong balls floating in water, and an experiment with a shielded candle flame. We were present for all these experiments together with Dr. Gadula, who gave the Japanese journalists lengthy, detailed explanations.

Before the crew left the apartment late in the evening, we installed a camera there and hooked it up to a VCR. The apparatus was to run nonstop until the Japanese departed from Poland and even (as we later arranged) for a week longer. It was turned off

55

only when Joasia was away from home (generally at school).

Aside from the fact that the whole project greatly inconvenienced the Gajewski household (after all, it's no fun being observed from morning to night), the basic problem was to find the right location for the camera. Obviously it could not scan the entire apartment. It also had to be firmly secured lest it be destroyed by a kinetic "onslaught."

We solved the first problem by placing the camera in the hallway, where it covered Joasia's bedroom and the kitchen. We made this decision on the basis of prior experience: the kinetic effects were usually concentrated in the hallway or the room where the girl slept. As for protecting the equipment, we fastened the camera to a wall and wedged the VCR between furniture. (In hindsight, we cannot help thinking that in view of the forces confronting us, our precautions were woefully inadequate, not to mention simple-minded.)

We finally left the Gajewskis' apartment around 9:50 pm and returned to our hotel by car. But Dr. Gadula spent the night there, not wanting to risk the drive back to his home in Tarnowskie Gory because of the late hour and the dense fog, which limited visibility to ten feet.

As Dr. Gadula recounted the next day, the first kinetic effects occurred at 10:45 p.m. (about an hour after we left the apartment) and continued with variable intensity until 11:08 p.m. This took place before the family went to bed.

The first object to move was a lipstick, followed by a coldcream jar (which had been in the bathroom), and then a knife the girl had bent a few days before. The trajectory of this last item was contrary to every known law of physics. When we subsequently retraced the course of events, we learned the knife had been placed (after being filmed) on a chest in the hallway, next to the front door. At the moment the kinetic effects began, nobody was near the knife. Propelled by an unknown force, it flew to the kitchen (meaning that the object executed a turn of at least seventy degrees in the air), rebounded against the wall over the kitchen sink and, changing direction again with a very sharp turn, headed toward the hallway and dropped on the floor close to the bathroom door. Since the knife's route or rather a segment of it was within range of the lens, there was a chance that the camera had captured part of its flight. (The other objects were outside the camera's field of view. And in Joasia's room, on which the camera was focused, nothing happened on the night of December 13.)

The initial viewing of the VCR cassette revealed nothing of interest. It seemed as though our hopes had been dashed. It was only on the third viewing that Yoshihiro Itoh, with a cameraman's practiced eye, called our attention to an odd, swiftly moving flash on the monitor. A rough estimate of the time that elapsed from the moment the camera was turned on and the beginning of the cassette recording indicated that the flash had been registered a few minutes after eleven o'clock.

We darkened the room, making it easier to observe the monitor, and gradually reversed and slowed down the frames. Finally, we managed to stop the image at the moment of greatest interest to us. We then saw that the effect noticed by the cameraman was not a single flash but rather two in succession. They resembled a pulsating line, which appeared suddenly on the hitherto motionless picture and later shifted to the right, changing color.

Might this have been a defect in the tape? Although Yoshihiro Itoh thought it unlikely, such a possibility could be ruled out only by special laboratory analysis, which could not be done until the crew returned to Japan. Assuming, however, that the knife really had flown, we made a rough drawing of its trajectory and concluded there ought to be some sort of mark on the spot where the object had struck the wall. After a brief search we found it: a small, shallow indentation in the wall, several inches above the sink. It looked as though it had been made by a sharp object.

A few weeks later we received important news from Japan: laboratory analysis had ruled out a defect in the VCR tape. The registered effect was therefore the image of some lightning-fast object. We say "some" because the object's velocity was so great that it was impossible to identify the object despite repeated enlargements. This closely matches accounts by eyewitnesses of kinetic effects occurring in Joasia's presence, who usually did not see objects flying but rather falling or striking an obstacle (only sometimes did they mention observing a blurred shape or a streak in the air for a split second).

Before the TV crew left, we agreed that if the laboratory analysis ruled out a tape defect it would be worth trying to determine at least the approximate velocity of the object by using the known speed of the frames as a basis for calculation. Regrettably, we did not receive such information. It seems the experts were unable to accomplish that task with the scanty and unreliable data at their disposal. But one thing is certain: though the object observed on the VCR screen is impossible to identify, it could not have been thrown by anyone. Otherwise, it would not have attained the incredibly high velocity in the visual recording (two successive flashes) of its trajectory.

Our several hours' visit to primary school no. 1 in Sosnowiec likewise proved fruitful. Although the improvised experiments there in which Joasia tried to extinguish a light bulb connected to a battery and move a stream of potassium permanganate in a flask of water ended in failure (as did her initial attempt to bend a spoon, which she finally accomplished in front of everyone when the camera was turned off), another of the scheduled experiments—the telepathic test—was a resounding success.

We administered this test in two stages, filming each one. In the first stage (the experiment was held in an empty classroom to help Joasia concentrate and to prevent schoolmates from possibly aiding her), she was to select geometric figures transmitted to her telepathically. The sender was one of the pupils, Wojciech Szewczyk, whom we chose for this role at the last moment. Of the twelve figures sent in this manner, Joasia correctly guessed ten.

To make the second stage harder, instead of a sheet of paper we used separate cards with drawn geometric figures. The sender this time was Joasia's teacher, Janina Ostrowski. This experiment also proved successful: out of the eight figures sent by the teacher (a triangle, rectangle, square, diamond, etc.), Joasia got seven right. Thus, in both cases her performance greatly exceeded chance probability.

Before leaving the school, we asked the class if any of the pupils would like to have Joasia's powers. There was total silence.

The boys and girls looked at each other hesitantly; nobody could muster up the courage to answer in the affirmative. We therefore rephrased the question: Was there anyone who definitely did *not* want to experience the unusual phenomena occurring around their classmate? Once again, silence.

During the Japanese crew's stay in Czeladz and Sosnowiec one more important event took place. While Joasia was being filmed, we heard the acoustical effects that had been mentioned by Drs. Franek and Gadula.

This happened on the evening of December 18. The previous day, writer Takashi Tachibana, who had to return to Japan earlier than the other crew members, decided to spend the night in the Gajewskis' apartment (this was after the "adventure" with the knife and the taping of the mysterious flashes, which coincided with the kinetic effects reported by the family and Dr. Gadula). Tachibana could not forgive himself for going to the hotel with us before ten o'clock that evening. The man was dying to see the unusual phenomena with his own eyes. He had no luck. But before turning in, he heard a strange noise (the family was asleep then). It was so strange that he could not identify or explain it. He asserted, however, that neither Joasia nor her parents had made it.

Mr. Tachibana also sensed that his hair was standing on end, not out of fear but because of the amazing electrification of the air that can sometimes be felt in Joasia's presence. You might call this a purely subjective phenomenon, for it has not yet been measured with instruments more credible than mere physical sensation. Yet it is a fact that once while we were filming the youngster, when we asked her to move her hand toward the head of one of the visitors (and Tachibana happened to be the person chosen), less than two minutes later his hair bristled. This observation, apart from its humorous aspect, confirmed that definite physical phenomena certainly do occur in Joasia's vicinity. After the experiment was over, Tachibana stroked his scalp distrustfully for a long time and was greatly intrigued by the whole matter: he was not, he claimed, subject to static electricity and nothing like that had ever happened to him.

But let's return to the acoustical effects. They occurred around six o'clock, immediately activating the camera and tape recorder. We felt a bit weary, which was to be expected after a series of failed experiments. Then Joasia, who was sitting motionless on the floor, suddenly began to "crackle." Every few seconds we heard distinct "static" that sounded like electrical discharges. It was focused at first around the teenager's feet, then seemed to rise into the air in her immediate proximity.

Recalling from the accounts of Drs. Franek and Gadula that such sounds often (though not invariably) preceded kinetic phenomena, we anxiously waited to see what would happen next. The acoustical effects gradually abated and finally disappeared altogether.

But a moment later something happened—something that undoubtedly bore all the characteristics of a definite, tangible physical phenomenon. For after changing places with Joasia (who had sat down in front of the camera again), the co-author of this book, Marek Rymuszko, felt a sharp pain in his temples, as though his head had suddenly been squeezed in a vise. Immediately afterward the energy that had caused this began to move down to his feet. There could be no question of mental suggestion here; the feeling was all too real, leading Dr. Gadula to intervene. At the same time, two members of the Japanese TV crew began to complain of severe headaches.

But that was not the only "adventure." Almost from the beginning of the Japanese telejournalists' stay in Czeladz, sound engineer Yoichi Hirai (one of whose duties was to monitor all the sophisticated technical gear) had been worried about the peculiar functioning of the equipment.

The glitches began with a lamp designed for 350 volts. In order to plug it into 220-volt outlets, it was necessary to use a transformer. Nonetheless, when we were filming experiments with Joasia in the Gajewskis' apartment, the transformer would not crank out more than 314-315 volts. Elsewhere (Joasia's classroom, the engineering school, while filming interviews with eyewitnesses to the phenomena) such a problem did not arise. Mr. Hirai, who had studied electronics, was quite perturbed over this and kept checking all the gear but found no signs of damage. He could not come up with a logical explanation for the considerable intermittent decrease in voltage.

Such phenomena as the sudden failure of electric devices (radios, tape recorders) in Joasia's presence had occurred before, as had the discharge of a battery in a digital watch. We should also recall the breakdown of an EKG apparatus during an examination of the girl in April 1983. Let's add—as if all this were not enough—that during the final stage of shooting the program on Joasia a large radio microphone the Japanese had brought with them started malfunctioning. Nobody was able to discover the reason for this either.

In exchange for film documentation of previous experiments (particularly Dr. Franek's biophysical experiments and Joasia's spoon-bending at the Institute of Metallography and Welding Technology at the Silesian School of Engineering) provided to the Fuji Television crew by the research team studying the girl, the visitors agreed shortly before their return to Tokyo to leave a camera along with a VCR and a large supply of cassettes in the Gajewskis' apartment for a week. Sadly, the apparatus failed to operate because of an unexpected event.

At 6 am on December 27, 1983, four days before the departure of the Japanese, all hell broke loose in the apartment. Light and heavy objects alike began hurtling through the air. One of them, a parlor lamp, hit Joasia in the face. At first, it was thought her nose might be broken. Luckily this proved not to be true but she was badly bruised and cut by flying glass. None of those kinetic effects showed up on tape: during these earth-shaking several minutes, the VCR fell on the floor and its cord was yanked out of the socket. (The camera, being fastened to the wall, remained intact.) When telephoning this information to the Japanese radio correspondent in Poland, Teruo Matsumoto (who had interpreted for the Fuji Television crew during its stay in Sosnowiec) said that Joasia's mother was nearly hysterical. Ewa was afraid she and her husband would have to pay for repairs to the expensive equipment. Luckily the damage did not prove serious, but both parents agreed it would be too risky to keep the equipment in the apartment any longer. It was therefore disassembled and shipped back to Tokyo via Warsaw.

The program on Joasia Gajewski and other sensitives (including the Japanese psychokinetics Matsuaki Kyota and Hiroto Yamashita) was broadcast in Tokyo on February 3, 1986. According to information we received from Japan, it was watched by some forty million viewers.

A bathroom faucet bent psychokinetically by Joasia during her stay in Rm. 309 at a sanatorium in Zakopane, Jan. 30, 1985.

Chapter 6
ROOM 309

One of the best-documented and most astounding episodes in the Joasia Gajewski story is the period she spent in late January and early February 1985 at the Jasinski Academic Rehabilitation Center in Zakopane. The phenomena that occurred during this period left so many physical traces and were witnessed by so many people that it seems impossible to deny their existence.

Joasia was invited to stay at the center by Dr. Gadula, who had taken a new job in early 1985 as director and chief physician of the student sanatorium[4] in Ciaglowka. He remained in charge of the girl's medical care, and because she, like her parents, had full confidence in him and would not hear of changing physicians despite the distance separating them, he proposed that Joasia spend her vacation at his institution.

Shortly before she departed for Zakopane, the Katowice newspaper *Wieczor* published on January 23, 1985, an article titled "The Eleven-Year-Old with Metal-Breaking Eyes." It turned out there was another girl in Sosnowiec, Agnieszka Gorski (her name was omitted in the text), four years younger than Joasia, with equally amazing powers. In the presence of newspaper reporters, she had bent two stainless steel spoons, among other items, by rubbing them.

Agnieszka's parents claimed their daughter could also (a) snap forks with her gaze; (b) bend nail heads; (c) stop, through mental effort, the motion of a silver earring dangling on a thread; and (d) attract or repel toys floating in water with her eyes. Reportedly she began to exhibit these abilities after watching *The Funfair*, a TV variety show on which Joasia Gajewski had appeared.

When Joasia was invited to display her talent on *The Funfair*,

---

4   In Poland, a sanatorium is an establishment for the medical treatment of people who are convalescing or have a chronic illness.

both Dr. Gadula and we tried to dissuade her parents from accepting the offer. First of all, the very name of the program, which featured rather low-grade sensationalist entertainment from Poland and abroad, did not inspire confidence. Second, after our long association with Joasia and observations of her generally unsuccessful encounters with the camera, we had strong reason to believe that nothing good would come of this venture. But because she was very eager to go to Warsaw (she had never been inside a TV studio), her parents finally consented.

Sad to say, our misgivings were borne out completely. Joasia, who was supposed to bend spoons in between performances by manic impersonators, contortionists, and rock bands, was distracted and dazed by the incessant hubbub around her (which the program's creators evidently meant to be a goal in itself). Consequently, the whole affair was a fiasco, whose bitter taste was not sweetened by the dinner we had together at our home after the show. To make matters worse, one of the *The Funfair* hosts encouraged viewers to try bending spoons on their own and report the outcome of their experiments to the TV station. And of course, mind-boggling revelations were not long in coming. One can safely say the bulk of them were products of the writers' imagination, mischievousness, or most often their desire to shine before the public at any cost.

These sarcastic comments are not directed at the eleven-year-old heroine of the news item in the Katowice *Wieczor*. We have never seen her in person, nor do we possess any information on which to base a judgment concerning her real or illusory powers. But it is a fact that after this article came out, Joasia, already upset over the failure of her TV appearance, became increasingly distraught. We sensed this in a phone conversation we had prior to her departure for Zakopane. Joasia was peevish and kept asking us what we thought about the newspaper story. Then she blurted out something we did not record verbatim, which is a pity, since in light of subsequent events her remark would take on an unexpected significance. What she said more or less was this: "Okay, then, I'll show everyone what *I* can do!"

Joasia was undoubtedly jealous of her "rival" and especially the publicity she had received. It also rankled her that people were saying, after the debacle at the TV studio, that even if she used to have some powers they were now obviously gone. The final indignity came from a member of the scientific council for the Ministry of Health. During a radio interview, when discussing the activity (or rather inactivity) of the departmental committee for alternative therapies, he stated it would also look into the matter of "that girl from Silesia who imagines something is flying around her." Although the connection between research on the efficacy of alternative therapies and the psychokinetic phenomenon associated with the Sosnowiec teenager seemed very tenuous, his words were spoken on the air, thereby exacerbating an already tense situation.

Joasia arrived at the Academic Rehabilitation Center in Zakopane on January 16, 1985. Dr. Gadula set her up in Room 309 on the third floor. Its double doors opened into the corridor and directly opposite them—this is a very important detail—was a communal bathroom with a shower.

Room 309, like the others, had standard hospital furniture and fixtures, including a sink with an overhanging shelf, a mirror, and a lamp on the nightstand. Other small objects had been removed per Dr. Gadula's instructions.

On the morning of January 30, 1985, the sanatorium patients and staff were alarmed by the sound of an explosion on the third floor. It came from Joasia's room. The acoustical effects, according to observers, did not last more than a few seconds. The doctors, nurses, and students who rushed to the room a moment later beheld the following scene.

The place looked as if it had been struck by a hurricane. The sink lay on the floor, smashed to pieces. One of its two supporting metal stanchions had been ripped off the wall; the other was buckled. The drainage pipe was severed at the elbow. The broken and strangely twisted faucet appeared to have been pounded with a sledgehammer.

For anyone who suspects the girl deliberately trashed her room once she was alone, we have just one question: How much strength and what tools would be needed to wreak such havoc in twenty seconds or less? It would also be interesting to learn how she could have yanked one of the sink's metal stanchions from the wall.

That day marks the most intense and destructive kinetic activity during Joasia's stay at the Academic Rehabilitation Center. But this was not the first such occurrence there; something happened two days earlier that borders on science fiction. If the eyewitness accounts are to be believed—and there is no reason not to—it would mean the end of all the recognized laws of physics.

We had not written about phenomena of this nature before (although we did keep reports about them on tape) because we considered them impossible to accept. The incident at the rehabilitation center in Zakopane convinced us they could not be dismissed any longer. What we are referring to is the passage of objects through solid matter.

Joasia Gajewski's parents, in conversations with us and members of the research team, frequently recounted incidents of this nature. Like the researchers, we did not give credence to such accounts, attributing them to the eyewitnesses' faulty perception or emotional upset. But the events at the sanatorium shook our convictions.

The two people who witnessed the January 28 incident were head nurse Krystyna Kolak and ward attendant Maria Wojtas-Opiela. They had been employed at the center for many years and had never shown an interest in psychic phenomena.

What transpired was this: Around 10 a.m. Krystyna Kolak went to Room 309, wanting to check with Joasia to see if she planned to go skiing. When she reached the door, she noticed Maria Wojtas-Opiela cleaning the lavatory across the corridor. She asked the ward attendant to wash the mirror there, which was a little dusty. The two women stood in the corridor near the closed double doors to Room 309. The lavatory door, however, remained open.

All of a sudden they heard a crash in Joasia's room, then the sound of breaking glass. The head nurse rushed inside to see what had happened. She noticed fragments of glass whirling in the air, which formed in a line, as if pulled by an invisible magnet, and

68

flew in her direction. Her apron was showered from top to bottom with glass. Meanwhile Joasia was sitting in a chair and, according to the head nurse, cried out: "Better not come in now!" The warning came too late—the woman had already been "attacked."

But that is not the most important aspect of this whole episode. Upon entering the room, Nurse Kolak saw that the floor was strewn with fragments of glass, so she automatically looked toward the sink and the shelf over which the mirror hung. The mirror was in its proper place. Almost at that very moment Attendant Wojtas-Opiela, who was in the lavatory, noticed that the mirror she was supposed to wash—which had been there just a few seconds before—had disappeared without a trace. Not a single piece of glass was on the floor. The object had simply vanished into thin air, ending up a split second later, shattered to bits, on the floor of Room 309, *whose door had been closed at the time*. To dispel any doubts, we should add that mirrors in patients' rooms were mounted in medicine cabinets over the sinks, whereas in lavatories they were installed on thick fiberboard sheets fastened to the walls with hooks. Among the shards of glass littering the floor in Room 309 lay a thick sheet of fiberboard...

All this defies logical explanation and smacks of sheer fantasy. A rationalist will no doubt be inclined to pooh-pooh this account as superstitious hokum, an old wives' tale. Yet we are dealing here with a concrete observation, which can be rejected only by accusing the witnesses of lying. Even if we assume for a moment that the girl did fabricate certain things, what could two mature, intelligent adults hope to gain by perpetrating such a hoax?

Can things pass through solid matter? Some physicists are willing to entertain the possibility based on the tunnel-quantum effect or the so-called slippage of atoms. (In "Appendix 1: Hypotheses," we cite the views of several experts who speculate on how this might happen.) As laymen we cannot judge whether the reasoning behind their arguments is correct, but we think it will be instructive now to hear the opinion of a scientist who is knowledgeable about electronics. Like many of the scientists we interviewed, Dr. K. wishes to remain anonymous.

An enlightened, broadminded man, Dr. K. believes that independent reports on the psychokinetic phenomena associated with Joasia Gajewski are so numerous that, like it or not, *we must accept such phenomena as real*. This also holds true for the passage of objects through solid matter. The explanation for this phenomenon, he thinks, may be less fantastic than it first appears. His argument in brief runs as follows:

Matter consists mainly of empty space. Of course, we don't perceive this with the naked eye, but that is precisely its essential nature. To take just one example: If the interstices were eliminated between the particles in a solid iron block with a volume of one square meter (or speaking figuratively, if the empty space inside it were removed) the block would shrink to a few square millimeters. That gives us a proper idea of the real ratio of solid matter to empty space in every substance.

The passage of objects through matter [Dr. K. emphasized that this was only speculation] may result from the shifting of some atoms in relation to others in the empty space surrounding them. Physicists have encountered a rather similar phenomenon in the case of superfluidity, a peculiar feature exhibited by some substances at temperatures close to absolute zero. Superfluidity is the passage of fluid practically without friction through narrow capillaries (thin tubes), interstices, etc. Hence, when such a fluid is set in motion within a capillary, it will remain in motion for a long time. The loss of friction at low temperatures must be considered a truly astounding phenomenon. We might compare it figuratively to the sliding of atoms on ball bearings.

Of course, this phenomenon is explained in very complex quantum theories. According to some of them, superfluidity simply creates specific, subtle bonds between atoms, which causes the atoms to move in an orderly manner and layers of fluid to shift without friction. Why then should we assume *a priori* that this is not possible in other situations, such as the passage of certain objects through matter? Perhaps in such cases too—for inexplicable reasons—the atoms of one body pass through the atoms of another without colliding with them.

In his conversation with us, Dr. K. cited one more graphic

example. If we observe a forest from a great distance, we perceive it as a solid, unbroken mass that looks impenetrable. But we need only approach the edge of the forest to find that there are spaces between the trees, allowing us to move freely and avoid obstacles. This may also be true of matter, which from the scientific viewpoint still contains many mysteries.

Let's go back to the incident of January 28. While collecting material at the rehabilitation center in Zakopane, we taped an interview with head nurse Krystyna Kolak. We sought to obtain as much information as possible from her about this and other occurrences during Joasia Gajewski's stay at the sanatorium. Here are excerpts from that interview.

Q. Had you ever seen so-called paranormal phenomena before?

A. No, never.

Q. How did you learn about Joasia Gajewski's special powers and the phenomena occurring around her?

A. It was in January 1985. There was a new director at the sanatorium, Dr. Eustachiusz Gadula. He told me once in a conversation that he was treating a girl in whose presence objects moved spontaneously. Of course I didn't believe him, I thought it was all in his imagination. But when Dr. Gadula said that by arrangement with Professor Magdalena Hanicki in Krakow the girl would be coming to us at the end of January for observation, I decided to pay careful attention to her. I simply wanted to find out the truth.

Q. Do you remember Joasia Gajewski's first day at the sanatorium?

A. Yes. Nothing peculiar happened then. Before the girl arrived, Dr. Gadula and I looked at the room on the third floor where she would be staying. I was supposed to remove any objects that might be destroyed by telekinetic phenomena. With that in mind, we cleared out all the dishes that patients receive for use at the sanatorium. I took the lamp off the nightstand and locked it away in the closet. I also put the radio and the potted plant on the floor, although Dr. Gadula said that wasn't necessary, because those kinds of things had never moved before during telekinetic occurrences. But I preferred not to take chances. I also wondered whether to take down the framed and glass-covered inventory list, but since that would have meant unscrewing it from the wall, I gave up the idea.

Q. What happened next?

A. As I said, nothing much the first day. But the following day, January 27, Dr. Gadula called me around ten in the evening. He said if I came to the ward I'd have an opportunity to hear Joasia "crackle." Supposedly that often precedes kinetic effects. I eagerly accepted his offer, especially as I live right next to the sanatorium, in the staff building.

Q. Did anything out of the ordinary happen that evening?

A. Yes. I saw for myself that the girl really did "crackle." It sounded like static and was very audible. We were sitting at the time in the director's office, then we moved to Room 309, where another nurse joined us. All of a sudden we noticed a light bulb socket on the floor, and a moment later some bits of glass. Normally the bulb on the ceiling was left on, and as I told you before, I had already locked away the bedside lamp in a closet. When I opened the closet with a key that I had in my pocket, we saw the bulb was missing from the lamp.

Q. Are you certain the bulb had been in it?

A. Of course, I checked it myself.

Q. Was this incident accompanied by any acoustical effects?

A. I don't recall anything like that.

Q. What else happened on the night of January 27 and the morning of January 28?

A. It may sound funny, but a metal handle from a cabinet in the corridor ended up in Room 309. We found it there in the morning. The inventory list fell off the wall too. I had wanted to take it down earlier but decided not to. The glass covering the list was shattered and the frame broken into several pieces.

Q. Was the cabinet in the corridor locked?

A. Yes.

Q. Are you sure?

A. Absolutely.

Q. Let's go back to the incident on January 28. Did you try to explain it as anything other than a paranormal phenomenon?

A. There's no other explanation. Right before the crash in Room 309 the mirror was inside the lavatory. Ward attendant Maria Wojtas-Opiela and I looked at it together. Otherwise, it wouldn't have made sense to talk about washing it.

Q. Are you sure the door of Room 309 was closed at the moment you heard the crash?

A. We were both standing in front of it, and I'm positive it was closed.

Q. Did you see anything at the critical moment that looked like a flying object or vibrations in the air?

A. I didn't notice. Besides, it all happened in less than a second. I just remember that a patient who was also in the corridor at the time of the crash showed us a strange mark on his arm. His skin appeared to have been cut by something sharp. He said the mark hadn't been there before.

Q. Are you aware of other telekinetic occurrences during Joasia Gajewski's stay at the sanatorium?

A. There were many, and we didn't record them all. Some of the items that wound up in Room 309 were a mirror from the fourth floor, a key from a locked cabinet in the duty-room, a pane of glass from a window in a landing, two lamps belonging to rooms 307 and 312 (in the former instance, only the shade), along with tableware, mugs, and glasses. Most of those objects were broken.

Q. You said that when you entered Room 309 you saw pieces of glass whirling in the air. Could you tell us more about that?

A. They were whirling very quickly in the middle of the room, about a foot and a half off the floor. The glass fragments flew toward me right after I opened the door. A few of them stuck to my apron; I brushed them off with my sleeve.

Q. You mentioned giving special attention to Joasia. What sort of attention?

A. We tried our best to spend as much time with her as we could so that she wouldn't feel lonely. With all the patients we have, though, it wasn't always possible.

Q. Based on your two weeks' personal observation and contact, what's your opinion of Joasia?

A. I think Joasia's a very nice girl. She was upset we had so much trouble with her. It made her feel bad that we had to keep removing glass and pieces of other objects from her room. I also noticed she felt ill for several hours after every incident. Her appetite was poor and she appeared weak, drowsy, and listless.

Q. Was there any other occurrence, besides the one with the mirror, that stands out in your memory?

A. A week or so after Joasia's arrival at the sanatorium, ward attendant Krystyna Strachera came to see me. She complained that she'd been conked in the head by a sugar bowl while cleaning Room 309 in Joasia's presence. She said she wouldn't clean there anymore.

Q. You're a nurse with many years' experience, a mature and knowledgeable person. What do you think of all this?

A. I can only state that everything I've said is true and I'm unable to explain the phenomena we witnessed. [end of recording]

We should add that Krystyna Kolak's account of the January 28 incident was fully corroborated by ward attendant Maria Wojtas-Opiela. She too had not seen the mirror move but only heard a tremendous bang, whereupon she discovered that the bathroom mirror she had intended to wash had disappeared and was lying shattered in Room 309.

In Joasia's medical chart at the sanatorium, under the heading "Diagnosis and Doctor's Recommendations" we find the entry "telekinetic powers." Other notations show that the patient's body temperature at the time it was measured (unfortunately no date is given for this) fell within the normal range (36.5C). Her pulse was 82; her blood pressure 100/65. The "History of Illness" section in the chart was replaced by a typewritten notation:

…the patient experienced frequent telekinetic
manifestations, which were witnessed by director
Gadula and head nurse Krystyna Kolak. The

patient complained of headaches during this time. Her axillary temperature was 39.9° and 39.8°C; her inguinal temperature–36.5° and 35°C. The following objects fell and broke: mirrors from the dresser and the lavatory, a sink, three bedside lamps from rooms 307, 312, and 309, the globe from an overhead light, a neon lamp, a windowpane in the corridor, and fuse box covers. Telekinetic phenomena subsequently occurred in the presence of Dr. Topor Madry and nurse Danuta Rozewicz. Mugs and plates continually fell and shattered. The patient's head was injured; there was blood on a switch plate. She left in good health.

Let's return to Room 309 for a moment. Amid the devastation that took place on January 30, 1985, one of the windowpanes drew attention (the sanatorium windows consisted of an outer and an inner pane). A closer inspection revealed that the inner pane was damaged, whereas the other remained intact. That in itself would not be remarkable were it not for one fact: in the middle of the inner pane, about where its diagonals intersected, there was a hole (which, according to one witness, looked as though it had been produced by a bullet). The hole's diameter was less than that of a knife–and a knife was stuck right between the window frames!

When the window pane was examined, it had no visible signs of damage, particularly longitudinal cracks. They appeared only the next day, and within a split second, when head nurse Krystyna Kolak walked up to the window in Joasia Gajewski's presence. The cracks radiated from the hole over the entire surface of the glass.

This was not the end of the inexplicable phenomena marking Joasia's stay at the Academic Rehabilitation Center in Zakopane. Here we shall describe the subsequent happenings on the basis of an account by Waldemar Sulek, then a junior in the Department of Economics and Business Management at the School of Engineering in Radom. He stayed at Ciaglowka from January

10 to February 5, 1985, referred by his school infirmary. He was twenty-four at the time.

Q. What did you see during your stay at the sanatorium?

A. On January 30, when there was an explosion in Room 309 that destroyed a sink, its stanchions, the windowpane, and other objects, I came to the spot a few minutes later. The whole room was littered with pieces of glass. Some of them had cut the girl, and a nurse had bandaged her hand. I took a number of photographs.

Q. You are speaking of the effects; we'd be more interested in your direct observations.

A. I understand. I simply wanted to say that seeing the physical effects gave me a good idea of what preceded them. Since those phenomena reoccurred later on, we sort of became used to them. I can say, for example, that they were always accompanied by loud noise, a din, which alerted us that something was happening. A classmate of mine, a psychology student, got Dr. Gadula's permission to spend the night with Joasia in her room. No objects moved then, but she said there were loud acoustical effects she couldn't explain.

Q. You said the phenomena reoccurred. Can you describe them?

A. On several occasions, various objects such as mugs and plates passed through solid matter. A small table lamp in another room on the same floor suddenly materialized in Joasia's room. What's most funny, a vial of the girl's urine, which was being kept in the lab and had a label with her name on it, inexplicably vanished from the lab and turned up broken in Room 309. The staff told us it would've been impossible for Joasia to gain access to the container after it was taken to the lab. I kept the pieces of the vial and the label as a souvenir.

Q. What made you decide to document those occurrences with notes and photographs?

A. After what happened on January 30, the goings-on at the sanatorium created quite a stir and generated a lot of discussion. We all realized we were dealing with something extraordinary that defied rational explanation and yet was undeniably real.

Q. Do you remember what took place on February 4?

A. Yes, I do, and very clearly, because the kinetic effects that night were probably the most intense of any during my entire stay at the sanatorium. As I was coming down from the fourth floor around eleven o'clock, I noticed a group of people gathered in front of the open door of Joasia Gajewski's room. The head nurse was among them. Joasia was in her pajamas. It turned out from her explanations that shortly after she had gone to bed "things started flying." In a few seconds, pieces of a ceramic bowl (which hadn't been in her room earlier) were lying all over the floor.

When leaving the room, we left the light on. Fifteen seconds or maybe half a minute later, it's hard to say exactly, we heard the next loud bang. We turned around immediately and ran inside. The girl was sitting as before on her bed, wrapped in a blanket. After looking around, we discovered that the light bulb over the sink was shattered. We talked with Joasia for a while, but she couldn't give us an explanation.

When we shut the door behind us again, there was another bang. This lasted only two or three seconds at the most, for we were literally standing by the threshold. We rushed back inside; she hadn't even had time to change her position. We soon found the cause of the sound: the bulb on the ceiling along with its globe was smashed to bits. As a result, the room was illuminated at that moment only by the light in the corridor.

We decided to put in a new bulb, but at first nobody could muster up the courage—we were afraid of new surprises. Finally, I took it upon myself. Using a flashlight brought by a nurse, I saw that some unknown force had damaged the old bulb so badly that its threaded metal base was torn out of the socket. How this happened is a total mystery to me: a moment before the explosion we all saw that the bulb was lit up and thus properly screwed in, plus it was covered by a globe. I anxiously shielded my eyes with one hand, and with the other I put in a new bulb. Luckily nothing happened. I remember that Dr. Gadula walked into the room then. He looked upset when I told him what happened. He had the girl moved to a room on the second floor, next to the nurses' office. The rest of the night was uneventful.

Q. During your stay at the sanatorium you talked a lot with Joasia Gajewski. What can you say about her?

A. I did talk a lot with Joasia, who was very popular with us, I mean the students being treated at the center. Everybody wanted to meet and quiz her. She must have found it a little tedious. Nonetheless, she readily answered all the questions and gave the impression of being a cheerful, humorous girl who seemed accustomed to her unusual situation. For example, we often teased her: "Joasia, what've you got planned for tomorrow, couldn't you let us know in advance?" Usually, our friendly joshing made her laugh. Such banter seemed to relieve the tension and uneasiness we all felt despite ourselves.

Of course, it was hard for Joasia to fit in with us at first, if only because of the difference in age and life experience. But that barrier quickly fell. I think the girl felt we were well disposed toward her, and that sort of gave her a psychological boost, for needless to say, not all the sanatorium personnel were happy about her "feats" and especially the damage they caused.

Q. You're an educated person and will soon receive your engineering degree. From that perspective, what's your opinion on the events you witnessed?

A. I've often pondered that myself. To my mind, they were proof of phenomena that are inexplicable to us but nonetheless real. I encountered them personally for the first time, and it was a fascinating adventure for me. Above all, no one can convince me now that they are just a figment of somebody's imagination. I think scientists ought to undertake a careful study of these phenomena, which would make it possible to formulate serious, objective hypotheses about them. Based on what my friends and I observed during our stay at the sanatorium, it's our firm belief that the inexplicable kinetic effects associated with Joasia Gajewski are undeniably real. The circumstances under which they took place rule out any possibility of a hoax. And therefore, science must tackle this problem. [end of recording]

For our part, we wish to add one piece of information to the cited accounts. In the sanatorium corridors, at a height of about seven feet, are electrical junction boxes. During one of the kinetic manifestations in Room 309, the tops of the boxes were torn off. Anyone wanting to cause such destruction by hand would have needed to use a ladder.

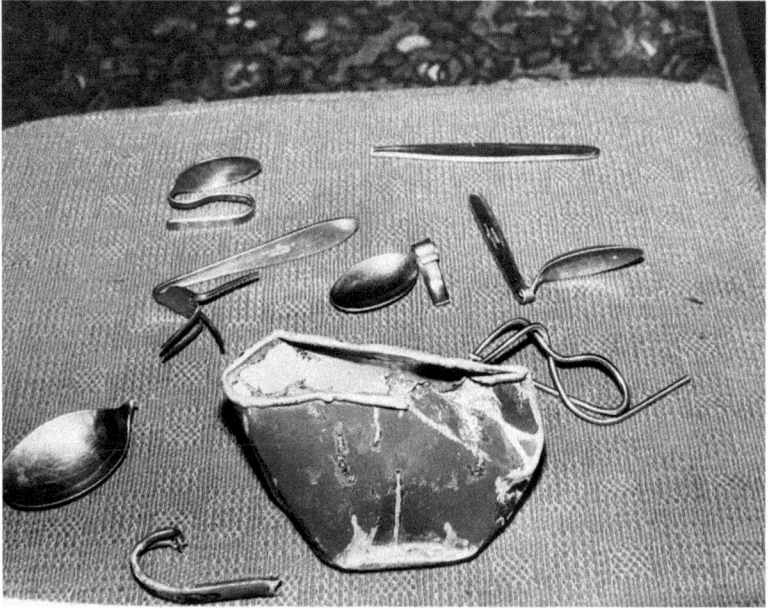

Twisted remnants of a flying pot that crashed into a wall in the Gajewskis' apartment, along with bent spoons and twisted forks.

Chapter 7
No Possibility of a Hoax

Gradually we are coming to learn more about the phenomenon of telekinesis, at least in its outward, tangible manifestations. At the same time, new doubts and questions are arising that pose a challenge to researchers.

Some puzzles could probably be solved were it not for ethical considerations. A person who is a subject of experiments cannot be treated like an inanimate object. He or she has the right to choose, to take an active part in the making of decisions that may affect his or her physical and emotional well-being.

In July 1983, during experiments conducted with Joasia Gajewski in Repty, researchers managed to generate kinetic effects through long preliminary irradiation of a room with ultraviolet rays. Having achieved this success, they were strongly tempted to keep repeating the procedure. But the quartz lamp used for this purpose made Joasia very ill; she felt dizzy, nauseous and drained of energy. With her parents' support, she refused to participate in these kinds of experiments.

The research done by specialists collaborating on Dr. Gadula's project seems to have properly integrated the sundry physical, medical, and psychological aspects of the phenomenon. Their joint conclusion ascribes it (implicitly) to the intense, atypical hormonal changes affecting the teenager's body. "It may well be," one expert speculates, "that the causative factor in this case is puberty." This hypothesis could surely be corroborated by detailed studies of her hormone levels. But that entails drawing numerous blood samples, which Joasia's parents would oppose because she has not tolerated such blood draws very well.

At one time it was thought that the kinetic effects had something to do with specific atmospheric conditions. They manifested fairly often, for example, in cloudy weather, especially right before a storm and atmospheric discharges. Later this hypothesis fell by the wayside, as such phenomena occurred—and continue to occur—regardless of the weather, temperature, and barometric pressure. Might they be produced by increased ionization of the air? The events in Zakopane would appear to indicate that this is a factor of some importance.

Joasia does not remember her dreams or at any rate does not talk about them much. Now and then she complains of kidney pains, but morphological studies have not revealed anything troubling. So is this merely a subjective feeling on her part or something else? Was the aseptic necrosis of a toe on her right foot several years ago somehow connected with the odd thermal spots noted around her feet?

In one experiment, Polaroid film was placed on Joasia's feet. The emanation effect on the film took the form of strange pink balls, which were partially concentrated under the base of the toes and heel. Was this a coincidence, or another sign that the girl emits a peculiar kind of energy, perhaps the same energy that caused her sutures to open so alarmingly right after her appendectomy on November 16, 1983?

There is a high-tension line near the Gajewskis' residence. Joasia feels dizzy and sick to her stomach whenever she passes under it. Doesn't this fact definitely refute the claims made by some experts that the girl's energy emissions lack the characteristics of an electrical or electromagnetic field?

We have stated that the spontaneous movement of objects is generally invisible owing to their tremendous velocity, and the motion can usually be perceived only at the moment an object collides with an obstacle. How, then, are we to explain the fact that when a glass of tea flew through the air, none of the liquid in it spilled? (Observed on May 12, 1983, in March 1984, and on January 13, 1986.)

A hypothesis formulated by Gerard Kubis, who is both a chemist and a physicist, seeks to elucidate this specific characteristic. He claims the girl affects particles of matter both separately and together, thereby producing an effect totally different than when a mechanical force is applied at a certain point. According to Kubis, the uniform action on all the atoms that undoubt-edly occurs does not disturb the structure constituting the whole (i.e., of a particular object). It is precisely this which accounts for the fact that no liquid spilled from a glass while it was in flight. This also causes tremendous acceleration, as much as 100 g. If an ordinary mechanical force were involved, the object's structure would collapse.

Faced with such conundrums, the only thing one can do is to conduct further studies.

The paper submitted by Dr. Gadula to the Ministry of Health and Social Welfare in October 1983 did have an impact. Although his proposal to establish a departmental program to study Joasia Gajewski failed to win acceptance, the report was forwarded to Professor Krystyna Bozkowa, director of the Institute of Mother and Child in Warsaw, along with a request for her opinion. As a result, an interdisciplinary scientific team was appointed to fur-ther research the phenomenon. It was headed by Professor Mag-dalena Halicki, an outstanding pediatrician from the Institute of Mother and Child (Krakow affiliate). The group also included Professor Jerzy Haber from the Institute of Catalysis and Physi-cal Chemistry of the Polish Academy of Sciences (Krakow affili-ate); Professor Andrzej Hrynkiewicz from the Institute of Nuclear Physics in Krakow and the Institute of Physics at Jagiellonian University; and engineer Grzegorz Zapalski from the Krakow Nuclear Research Institute.

On February 10, 1984, all four members of the team partici-pated in the first series of experiments with Joasia Gajewski at the Institute of Physics at Jagiellonian University. Their findings are contained in a report submitted on February 18, 1984, to Profes-sor Krystyna Bozkowa. In view of the significance of certain opin-ions expressed in this document, we think it should be presented here in full. We have italicized some passages for emphasis.

> In reference to the request from the Ministry of Health and Social Welfare for an evaluation of the accounts in Dr. Eustachiusz Gadula's letter that describe bioenergetic phenomena associated with the girl Joasia Gajewski, we

wish to state the following.

1) On February 10, 1984, an experiment was conducted at the Institute of Physics at Jagiellonian University in which the subject bent a number of stainless-steel spoons by rubbing them with the fingers of her right hand. Immediately after they were bent, the spoons did not show a rise in temperature. *Independent tests have ruled out the possibility of a hoax* involving the use of pressure to bend the objects.

Throughout the experiment we monitored the girl's physical condition, measuring her respiration and pulse rate, and attempting to detect possible magnetic and mechanical fields. The spoon-bending was accompanied by a considerable increase in her pulse rate (up to 140/min.) and her respiration (up to 30-40/min.). During the three-hour experiment we observed arrhythmia of the subject's pulse and respiration. No marked disturbances of the magnetic field were noted.

2) Our findings indicate *that we are dealing with a phenomenon wherein a living organism affects the objects surrounding it in a manner that cannot be explained on the basis of the known laws of physics.* This seems to be a most intriguing problem, and it calls for special study.

In connection with the aforementioned facts, we propose that an interdisciplinary research program be established, which would include experiments aimed first at discovering the laws governing this phenomenon and then at elucidating its mechanism. This program could be financed within the framework of an interdepartmental program coordinated by the Institute of Mother and Child.

Finally, we deem it advisable that before any systematic studies are undertaken, the family must pledge in writing to collaborate with the research team.

[signed]

Jerzy Haber, Institute of Catalysis and Physical

Chemistry, Polish Academy of Sciences, Krakow

Magdalena Halicki, Institute of Mother and Child, Krakow affiliate

Andrzej Hrynkiewicz, Institute of Nuclear Physics in Krakow and Institute of Physics at Jagiellonian University

Grzegorz Zapalski, Engineer, Krakow Nuclear Research Institute

We think this document ought to convince even the greatest skeptics that the phenomenon does exist, at least insofar as it could be observed by the physicists and physicians taking part in the metal-bending experiment. During this experiment, incidentally, the usual surprises occurred. While Joasia was bending a spoon, for example, the monitor of the American electrocardiograph to which she was hooked up suddenly stopped operating. (This was not the first such incident—the same thing occurred with one of the early EKG tests in April 1983.) What's most curious, however, is that at the same moment another monitor (constructed by Grzegorz Zapalski of the research team), which was connected to a sensitive detector to pick up weak physical fields, exhibited some odd vibrations.

"I can't describe them precisely," said Mr. Zapalski. "They lasted only ten seconds at the most and then disappeared, so there wasn't enough time to record them. Besides, at that moment we were using an oscilloscope, not an oscillograph, which would have made such recording possible. Because our data were insufficient when we began the experiment, I tuned the monitor randomly and didn't have time to readjust it to the right frequency. But what I did observe on the screen strikes me as extremely interesting."

"When studying something new," remarked Professor Magdalena Hanicki, a warm, gracious, and truly broadminded person, "we must abandon the prejudices and mental blinders we bring with us from our academic training or profession. I believe such an approach is particularly essential in Joasia's case."

Taking advantage of our visit to Professor Hanicki, we questioned her about various matters.

"What happened to the monitor during the experiment on February 10?"

"Well, it simply broke down, which surprised us because it had been working fine until then. I'm a little afraid now to use the device in the next experiments. It's worth millions of zlotys and supposed to be used for sick children."

"In your report on the experiment of February 10, 1984, you stated that the phenomena you observed were real and could not be explained on the basis of the known laws of physics. It took courage to put forward such a conclusion."

"I think it's a question of honesty more than anything else," said Hanicki. "But we did discuss it a long time beforehand. I as a physician, for example, know little about physics and maybe least of all about catalysis and physical chemistry. Thus, the exchange of views between the physicists on the research team was fascinating, though often incomprehensible to me. For my part, I thought it most important to discuss whether the girl was a generator, transformer, or simply a good conductor of energy (perhaps she converts one form of energy into another). There are many indications, however, that this is some unknown type of energy. Remember, electrical energy itself was discovered fairly recently, so it seems quite probable that unidentified forms of energy do exist. We therefore have to eliminate any possibility that previously known and described forces are operating in this particular case. Highly sensitive and reliable equipment must also be found to fully register the phenomenon.

"The experiments in question," added Professor Hanicki, "should be held in specially adapted rooms. I even considered putting up Joasia in my clinic and driving her from there to the physics institute. But after what happened in Zakopane, I felt apprehensive. For certain reasons I can't afford to have any 'miracles' taking place. I do have sick children in the ward, after all."

"You used the word 'miracles.' Was that deliberate?"

"Let me be perfectly clear. By signing the report, we confirmed the existence of the phenomenon. Because we espouse a strictly scientific approach, we can't deny the facts. But I'm only human, and when I said 'miracles' I was expressing our subjective, everyday perception of the whole phenomenon."

"What do you think the prospects are for future studies on Joasia?"

"It's not a simple matter. We were unable to incorporate the problem in a departmental research program because the five-year plan is ending just now and nothing can be squeezed into it. Maybe it'll be possible later on, but that won't resolve the matter completely. The team includes eminent physicists who often travel abroad, so it's hard to guarantee their simultaneous presence at experiments. I've already mentioned the need to provide suitable conditions for the experiments. I think it's no accident, for example, that the manifestations were so violent in Zakopane, where the air is highly ionized. This could be a meaningful factor. In addition, objects in the girl's room should be carefully inventoried and kept to a minimum to eliminate the possibility of errors in perception. And not only inventoried but weighed. Doctor Gadula claims, for instance, that one of the mugs was much heavier. But that's a purely subjective opinion, since the mug hadn't been weighed earlier. Recently I got a call from a physicist I know, a lecturer named Szczepanski from Warsaw, who suggested we take Joasia back to Zakopane in the summer and repeat the experiments under controlled conditions. To me, the most important thing is to establish the research guidelines."

We also asked Professor Hanicki for her opinion on psychic phenomena.

"On this subject I'm cautious but open-minded."

[...]

"This phenomenon must be studied as objectively as possible. Third-person accounts, even if they're true, cannot constitute an adequate basis for scientific verification. To satisfy scientific criteria a completely different approach is needed. For example, in our future experiments we would like to eliminate spoons and replace them with bars with known parameters. And if we find, after Joasia has bent a few dozen of those bars, that their metallurgical properties have changed, this will be a statistically significant effect from which one can draw appropriate conclusions."

Adds engineer Grzegorz Zapalski: "Every day of our lives we are surrounded by physical fields—electrical, magnetic, electromagnetic, etc. Although we don't feel them, they pass through us continually, affecting our bodies and environment. In research on Joasia Gajewski these forces must be reduced to a minimum. […] Otherwise, we'll never be sure whether or not the results were skewed by extraneous factors."

Apart from technical difficulties, there is always the problem of the researcher's own preconceived notions and inner resistance to new ideas. Julian Ochorowicz, the Polish philosopher and psychologist, once said that nothing is more conducive to progress than discoveries at variance with the prevailing theories. It would seem that where complex physical and mathematical models are concerned, philosophy has little to contribute. But with the rapid development of the exact and natural sciences, which are constantly revising paradigms long regarded as unshakeable, Ochorowicz's dictum has become more relevant than ever.

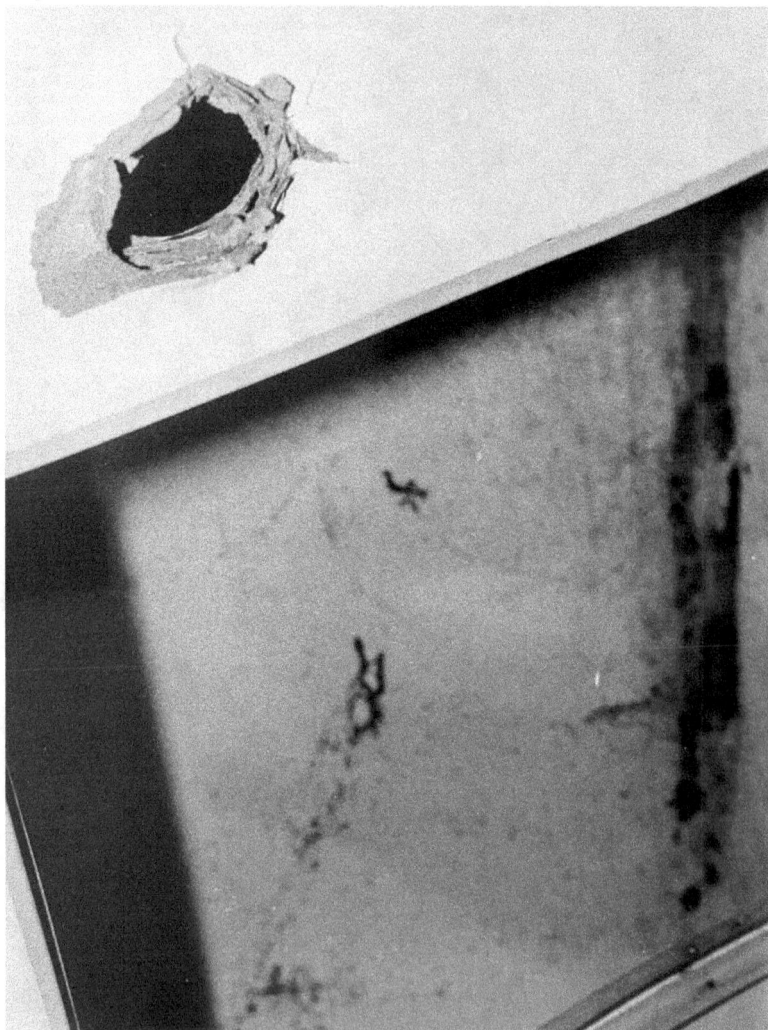

A hole in a door in the Gajewski family's apartment in Czeladz, caused by a bottle flying at a tremendous velocity.

Chapter 8
A FLURRY OF OTHER POLISH POLTERGEIST CASES

We would be remiss if we failed to mention that between 1983-1986 some twenty reports about other poltergeist cases and their psychokinetic agents appeared in the Polish press. Here is an abridged account of them.

Next to the Sosnowiec phenomenon the most celebrated case of psychokinetic effects was in Sochaczew, at the Sokol home. They began in December 1983 with banging on the walls and spontaneous movement of household objects (drawers falling out, glasses of water overturned, etc.). The media devoted much coverage to these happenings. Since we were in Sochaczew ourselves, we would like to share a few thoughts on the matter.

During our visit to the Sokols we interviewed not only thirteen-year-old Joanna Sokol (around whom the phenomena were apparently concentrated) and her mother Anna, but also several people outside the family who had witnessed these occurrences.

Let's start with Dr. Roman Bugaj, who investigated the Sochaczew case for the Warsaw Psychotronic Association. He presented his initial findings at the symposium "Psychotronics 85" and elaborated on them in a conversation with us and in a two-part article in *Tygodnik Demokratyczny*.

Dr. Bugaj stated that he, along with the president of the Psychotronic Association Lech E. Stefanski and several others, had observed the following kinetic effects in Joanna Sokol's presence:

1. While the girl was passing through the kitchen, a shoe lying in the corner suddenly rose into the air and followed her;

2. A tin pot spontaneously slammed into a wall;

3. A metal shovel lying on the floor flew several feet and landed near the kitchen;

4. A china plate "took off" at once from the table and, flying right below the ceiling, smashed into the opposite wall;

5. A fur cap left on a bed zoomed into the kitchen, hitting Dr. Bugaj in the face;

6. When the cap was put back on the bed, it streaked into the kitchen again;

7. A glass of hot tea flew past an eyewitness, missing his head by a few inches but splashing his suit, then shattered against the sideboard;

8. Two stones that could not have been thrown by anyone fell into an upstairs room through a narrow crack in the door;

9. Lech Stefanski was struck on the head by a spontaneously propelled Rubik Cube.

The majority of these phenomena occurred either in daylight or in bright electric light. The objects flew rapidly, with a distinctive whizzing or rustling sound.

When Joanna Sokol rubbed an aluminum spoon with one finger, its handle broke, according to Dr. Bugaj, but other cutlery made of stainless steel was bent.

One man who observed most of these effects was police lieutenant Leszek Franaszek, who took part in these experiments at the researchers' request. When the phenomena first occurred (in late 1983), he witnessed the spontaneous movement of a TV set, which flew ten or twelve feet and smashed into a wall.

A chemist who traveled to Sochaczew frequently, Gerard Kubis, told us that in September 1984, just as Joanna Sokol and he were entering an empty room, a flowerpot on the balcony rose into the air, zoomed past his head, and shattered against the opposite wall.

The eyewitnesses' educational background, professional reputation, experience, and perceptiveness make these accounts very credible. For our part, we will just add that based on a personality test we administered to Joanna Sokol during our interview with her, she seems to be considerably above average in intelligence. This fact may well prove significant in understanding her case.

Continuing the list of similar phenomena exhibited by others between 1983-1986 and reported in the Polish press:

Eleven-year-old Grzegorz Osmolek from Konin. If one can believe the stories about him in the press, he also caused spontaneous movement of objects (toys, dishes, a radio-cassette player, even a washing machine and heavy furniture), some of which "assaulted" the boy (stones would "pop up" from the ground and strike his head). Locked doors opened automatically in his presence.

Twelve-year-old Artur Matura from Jastrzebi Zdroj could "make the air drip." His family's apartment was permanently flooded; water flowed from ceilings and walls, ruining the furniture, although plumbers had come and shut off the water supply. Water poured from the ceilings even when the boy (on doctors' orders) was tied up and placed on a sofa. These inexplicable occurrences were observed by reporter Grazyna Kuznik for the Katowice journal *Tak i Nie* ("A Strange Phenomenon," no. 39/85).

Eleven-year-old Agnieszka Gorski from Sosnowiec (see the chapter "Room 309") bent spoons and nails with her eyes, attracted toys floating on water, and stopped watches.

Nine-year-old Agnieszka Stopczyk from Lodz (see the chapter "Comprehensive Studies").

The case of Agatka from Ostroda (reported in the magazine *Warmia i Mazury*, July 15, 1985, which regrettably provided few details about the girl featured in the story). According to the author, she could bend spoons and break aluminum tableware with her eyes. Fuses also blew in her presence.

The phenomena in the Kudrys family's apartment in Myszkow. If accounts describing them are accurate, the kinetic effects would be the most intense ones recorded thus far. They included rapid movement of objects (sometimes through matter), constant "tossing" of eggs (some of which were boiled in mid-air), and numerous explosions. Among the eyewitnesses were members of the local militia (who saw an aquarium move spontaneously) and Iwona Chudzinska, a reporter for the weekly *Rzeczywistosc*. She observed the flight of an egg, a Christmas tree ornament, and an onion ("Spirits in Myszkow" in *Rzeczywistosc*, no. 9/1986). These effects occurred both in the presence of a large number of people and when nobody was home, so they did not appear to be connected with a specific individual. After the happenings in their apartment were verified, the Kudrys family was relocated to a hotel.

We cannot comment on the above cases, since we did not investigate them personally. We simply want to stress the need for caution with respect to such reports, and especially the need for thorough documentation. Only meticulous recording and examination of the facts will make it possible to determine whether a given phenomenon is real or the product of a cleverly contrived hoax.

We address this demand not only to our fellow writers but also–and perhaps primarily–to ourselves. For inasmuch as we affirm the existence of psychic phenomena, we feel obligated to adopt a particularly critical perspective toward this subject— which does not mean an adamantly negative view regardless of the facts!

The need for such a stance is clearly illustrated by a story we wish to relate here, believing it offers valuable lessons of a general nature. Our account will leave out the name of the place where the events took place as well as the name of the individual associated with them. For it is not our intention to hurt anyone, and moreover the person concerned is a minor who still has enough time to reflect upon her behavior and become a decent human being once she reaches maturity.

And so, in June 1983, shortly after publication of a lengthy article weighing the initial results of experiments with Joasia Gajewski, we received a letter whose author described an equally intriguing case of psychokinesis at the opposite end of Poland. It purportedly involved a twelve-year-old girl living in a small town in Szczecin Province.

In deciding to look more closely into the alleged phenomenon, we were principally motivated by the consideration that the letter came from a juvenile court judge, hence someone who was undoubtedly credible. We therefore got in touch with her, requesting as many details as possible. Our correspondence lasted almost ten months. Here are the essential facts.

According to the account of Judge F., the troubles with twelve-year-old Renata K. (a pseudonym) began sometime in mid-1983. [Note the striking congruence of dates: the events in

94

Sosnowiec had occurred shortly before and were accompanied by a spate of items in the press devoted to them.] Members of Renata's family recounted that the girl could shatter a glass container by holding her hand a few inches away, and windowpanes would rattle whenever she came near. Objects, including pieces of furniture, were often said to move spontaneously in Renata's presence. These effects would manifest in the nighttime and the early morning hours; as one letter claimed, "When Renata goes to bed, the sofa shakes and makes loud thumping noises, so it's impossible for her and the rest of the family to fall asleep."

According to another letter (dated January 27, 1984), toward the end of December 1983, while with a small group of people among whom were acquaintances of Judge F., the girl easily slid across the floor a table standing ten feet away and even levitated it a few inches. Supposedly it was a heavy oak table that when fully extended could seat twelve persons.

Most intriguing, however, was the final letter from Judge F. (dated May 30, 1984), which presented the results of her personal observation. Basically, it was this message that persuaded us to make a trip to the town of B. Here are some excerpts:

Last Saturday night when I was in B., I stayed at Renata's home [...] Based on what I saw, I'm justified in thinking that you [the letter was addressed to Marek Rymuszko] ought to go there at once, especially since the girl's mother and grandmother feel overwhelmed by everything that is going on there, and they hope for a calm, straightforward explanation of these phenomena.

My observation of the girl was all the more difficult because I felt very ill in her presence, kind of dazed [...] What did I see with my own eyes? Well, Renata lifted a heavy oak table, or to be more precise, one side of it in such a manner that the table stood up on two legs and the top was tilted toward the floor at a 70-degree angle. It remained like that for a long while, and no one except the girl was able to force it back to a normal position (I tried it myself).

On top of Renata's desk, a toy fire truck rode around beeping its horn and raising its ladder. Her mother also told me Renata was able to open the curtains on the window from a distance of several yards, and an accordion in the next room could play by itself. The girl also has the ability to read a card written by another person and placed in a sealed envelope [...]

But all that is nothing compared to what's been happening lately. Renata is reportedly "materializing" a hand—a living, warm, and moving one—and claims she'll soon be able to materialize an entire figure. She can likewise "materialize" and then "dematerialize" various items, such as a sweater. I wasn't present when the sweater was "dematerialized," but I did take part in finding it.

At the end of the letter, Judge F. conveyed a request by the girl's mother to come as soon as we could, adding that a parapsychology club had expressed interest in Renata.

To be quite honest, certain things about this correspondence aroused our suspicion or at any rate made us very cautious in judging its credibility. We particularly disliked the mystical aura surrounding the alleged phenomena (i.e., the house was said to be haunted by a mysterious "sprite") and the fact that they manifested only in the evening or late at night. After all—please excuse the sarcasm—it shouldn't matter to a ghost when it makes an appearance! Nevertheless, trying to remain level-headed and unbiased, we concluded that the case deserved a closer look; we could not rule out, for example, that the kinetic effects were real and that an esoteric interpretation was being imposed on them. Consequently, in July 1984 we set out for B.

Unfortunately, our suspicions were fully confirmed: the story about Renata K.'s "miraculous" powers turned out to be utter nonsense. Amazingly, certain people attending "seances" with the youngster were so gullible that they mistook obviously staged effects for real phenomena. To some extent this is excusable, for the witnesses' powers of observation were thrown off by the dim lighting. Our supposition had proved correct: this was a key factor.

As for the table (which indeed was large and heavy), it really did rear up on two legs, but only because the girl supported it from underneath using her abdomen. Incidentally, she pulled off this stunt with great skill, which might fool a less perceptive observer into believing the table had tilted on its own toward the floor at a sharp angle. In this instance, the youngster displayed a truly remarkable familiarity with the laws of physics by finding the table's center of gravity and the very spot where the "application" of mechanical force yielded the best result.

We did not see a toy fire truck cruising independently around a desk, but looked at identical toys in a store. Setting them in motion is as simple as can be: you need only rub the vehicle's wheels several times against a smooth, hard surface, and the gear tooth mechanism inside will engage and start running.

The "materialization" and "dematerialization" of various items were likewise the result of obvious tricks made possible by gaps in the observers' perception, while the "spontaneously" playing accordion, as one can easily guess, was greatly "assisted" by a sound-recording tape.

The tale about the hand turned out to be the most idiotic one of all. The hoax in this instance was exceedingly crude: the "materialized" hand belonged to Renata's kid sister hiding near the sofa. The various canned sound effects (knocking and crackling) were equally primitive.

As for the telepathy tests we had prepared in advance (including a card with sentences in a sealed envelope), the girl failed to pass a single one.

This story might seem to be an argument for total rejection of paranormal phenomena, which some claim are always and solely the result of fraud. We firmly contend, however, that when a particular case contains an element of psychological or manual trickery (both of which often go together), an astute observer employing rigorous research methods is bound to expose it sooner or later without much difficulty.

Joasia with authors Anna Ostrzycka and Marek Rymuszko, 1986.

Chapter 9
A FINAL NOTE

1986

Having spent many hours in conversation with Joasia Gajewski over a period of more than three and a half years, we are coming to realize how much she has changed during this time. Writing about her in 1986, we should no longer refer to her as a "girl," for on March 25, 1986, Joasia turned sixteen. She has matured both physically and emotionally.

When we asked Joasia in the summer of 1983 what she thought of the phenomena that had been part of her life for several months, she replied: "I never know when they're going to happen, but I'm not afraid of them anymore. You can get used to anything." Now, three years after that conversation, she seems to be weary of these incidents. And as time goes by, her situation is becoming increasingly difficult.

The kinetic effects still occur irregularly and with varying degrees of intensity, but with certain new characteristics. Above all, they are beginning to follow the teenager and manifest more frequently outside the family apartment. What's worse, some of them turn out to be quite unpleasant for Joasia herself.

We have often urged the Gajewskis to keep a sort of diary in which to record the individual phenomena along with their exact date, hour, and a brief description. Unfortunately, this has proved impossible, largely because of the nervousness of Mrs. Gajewski, who is completely frazzled after every such incident. Thus the dozen or so observations presented below come from our own chronological notes, which in turn are based on eyewitness accounts (by family members as well as third persons) primarily from 1983-1986.

On June 17, 1983, among numerous objects set in motion at the same instant and smashing into walls, there was a medicine bottle, which Andrzej Gajewski managed to catch in mid-flight. He said the glass was so hot it burned his fingers, but it soon cooled off. This account seems all the more convincing as many people have spoken of the high temperature of certain objects immediately after their flight.

On September 23, 1983, at six o'clock in the morning, there was a veritable kinetic explosion in the apartment. Various items, mostly tumblers, pots, dishes, cosmetics, shoes, and cutlery, hurtled with such tremendous velocity that careful observation was out of the question. The phenomenon lasted four to six minutes. The extent of the destruction is evident in photographs taken several hours later by personnel from the Documentation Center at the Gliwice School of Engineering. They show hundreds of glass fragments littering the floor, marks on the walls and doors, and a great deal of other damage.

On October 1, 1983, Dr. Eustachiusz Gadula witnessed the paranormal movement of two scissors in the Gajewski apartment. They flew so quickly it was impossible to observe them.

On April 5, 1985, around one o'clock in the afternoon, Joasia phoned us from Czeladz to say she was home alone and "things had started flying." Over the phone, we could hear a cacophony, which sounded like objects whizzing through the air and slamming into walls. To produce such acoustical effects (given that she was standing with the phone in her hand at that moment) there would have had to be at least two other people in the apartment. Right after we finished talking to Joasia, we called Ewa and Andrzej Gajewski to verify her story. Both of them were at work.

On the night and early morning of August 8-9, 1985, while Joasia was sleeping with her mother, another kinetic manifestation occurred. One of the hurtling objects, a glass, struck Ewa Gajewski in the head, leaving a small bruise and a lump.

On August 30, 1985, all faucets in the apartment were bent in the space of twenty seconds. Shortly after they were replaced, the new ones also got bent.

On September 4, 1985, the sink was ripped from the wall, together with one of its metal stanchions (the second one got twisted).

On October 1, 1985, during an afternoon show at the Muza movie theater in Sosnowiec where Joasia had gone with her friends Szymon Siedlecki and Wojciech Dudala, pieces of glass suddenly flew toward her and cut her cheek. Nobody knows how the glass got into the theater.

On March 8, 1986, while Joasia's classmate Joanna Potepa was visiting her, something very dangerous happened. A fifteen-pound power drill left by Joasia's father in the hall suddenly rose in the air, flew about ten feet, smashed into the bathroom door, and landed in the tub, where a blanket was soaking. The girls were in a bedroom at the time and nobody else was home.

On March 21, 1986, when Joasia was leaving the apartment with a friend, she was hit in the back by a fork. Other flying objects struck the walls.

On April 10, 1986, Joasia came down with a very high fever (41.5°C), which lasted two days. During this time she lost consciousness. Doctors from the emergency medical service who were summoned several times were baffled and unable to diagnose her condition. The high temperature was accompanied by intensified kinetic effects and a totally new phenomenon: water dripped from the ceilings and walls, soaking the beds, carpets, and many pieces of furniture. This continued even after the water supply to the apartment had been shut off.

During our final visit to Czeladz (in the fall of 1986), we taped interviews with others who had witnessed kinetic effects. In the majority of incidents the phenomena were seen simultaneously by at least two persons.

Here is a statement by Malgorzata Formicka, a first-year student at a nursing school with whom Joasia started classes on September 1, 1985: "A few days after the beginning of the school year I was going with Joasia and other girls to the swimming pool. As we were walking down the corridor on the ground floor of the building, we suddenly heard a loud noise. We noticed pieces of glass lying on the floor near a window. We don't know how they got there, since the windowpane wasn't broken."

Agnieszka Grygiel, a student at the same nursing school, said: "A few weeks ago, I don't remember the exact date, I observed a glass and a cup flying in Joasia Gajewski's room. The glass hit our classmate Joanna Potepa in the head."

Said Joanna Potepa: "I often saw various objects flying in Joasia's presence. For example, during a recent visit to our friend Renata Beben, a glass suddenly took off and conked me on the head. Another time, when Joasia and I were leaving her apartment, a knife hit me in the back."

Szymon Siedlecki, a student at the liberal arts lyceum in Bedzin, said: "I was with Joanna and a friend of ours, Wojciech Dudala. We saw various things fly, including a bottle that hit a wall. When Joasia was leaving the apartment with us, a bottle of tonic drops flew behind her into the landing. A similar thing happened when I went to see Joasia at the hospital where she did volunteer work as part of her studies. As we were walking down the corridor, we heard a loud bang. After looking around we saw a vial, which had struck the banister and shattered. The cleaning woman got angry at us because she thought we were playing tricks on her. Just then a bottle of medicine flew behind Joasia and fell on the floor. We immediately took it to the treatment room but the nurse refused to accept it."

Said Joanna Potepa: "While we were doing volunteer work at the hospital, my classmates and I saw a bottle suddenly fall on the floor. This happened near the neurology ward; it seemed as if the bottle had materialized from the ceiling."

We questioned Szymon Siedlecki, another witness: "Can you describe the phenomena you observed in Joasia Gajewski's apartment on February 17, 1986?

His reply: "Things were flying around 'normally,' as always. I just remember that the faucets in the kitchen and bathroom got bent then."

We should mention that the teachers of the three girls whose statements we cited above consider the girls intelligent or highly intelligent. Nor have they ever heard them tell wild stories or noticed any inclination on their part to do so.

Joasia has a good reputation at her new school. When she was admitted to the nursing school after passing the entrance exam, nobody associated her with the stories that had appeared in the press two and a half years earlier and that had already been forgotten. This is not surprising, for "Gajewski" is a common surname and her parents preferred to keep her out of the limelight.

But her identity could not be concealed for long. The first person to guess her identity was Joasia's current teacher, Jolanta Wolniak, who, like Janina Ostrowski at the primary school, kept an eye on her student. The last one to find out was the school principal, Leszek Lasota. Fortunately, he is flexible and fully understands the need for an individual approach to such an unusual charge. For his part, he had only a single request: he wanted Joasia to bend a spoon in his presence so he could keep it as a souvenir. This experiment, carried out in the principal's office with us and two teachers present, succeeded despite Joasia's obvious trepidation. Immediately afterward she returned to nursing class, where the girls practiced changing the underwear of a bedridden patient and disinfecting beds with Lysol. Joasia is majoring in nursing and intends to pursue a career in this field.

Will the phenomenon associated with Joasia Gajewski of Silesia continue for long? There is no one today who can answer this question. If, as some people maintain, the kinetic effects are in fact due to turbulent hormonal changes within her body, the unusual phenomena may cease at the end of puberty. The situation may also turn out differently, as one can see from such examples as the Japanese sensitives Masuaki Kiyota and Hiroto Yamashita. The latter possibility is all the more plausible in light of Dr. Miroslaw Harciarek's interesting and cogent hypothesis linking the phenomenon to the specific transfer he observed between Joasia's cerebral hemispheres during his experiments with her. We might add that this view corresponds to the opinion expressed by Dr. Wolfgang Howald from the University of Muenster. In our interview with him in September 1985, Dr. Howald noted "unparalleled, very high level of coherent electrical activity in the cerebral hemispheres" registered in experiments with individuals who exhibit psychic powers.

The observations made during the more than forty months that have elapsed since the initial appearance of the odd effects around Joasia Gajewski have failed to resolve the issue. It is even difficult to say whether they have clarified it in any meaningful way. But they have contributed to our knowledge of the phenomenon and enabled us to record its outward manifestations with a fair degree of precision. This is a great step forward, but still not enough to warrant categorical interpretations and conclusions. One thing is certain: in light of the materials furnished by the experiments and tests conducted in this period, it would be quite pointless to question the very existence of the phenomenon.

The renowned Hungarian biochemist and Nobel Prize winner in 1937, Albert Szent-Gyorgyi, wrote: "Physics is the science of probabilities, whereas biology is the science of improbable phenomena. The living organism operates on the basis of reactions that are statistically improbable."

Our story of the Sosnowiec phenomenon breaks off in mid-1986.

1989

Joasia Gajewski turned nineteen on March 25, 1989. She still attends the nursing school and is graduating this year. Since September 1989, in accordance with the school curriculum, she has been serving along with her classmates as an intern in the general surgery ward at the hospital in Czeladz. She changes dressings, administers medicines and intravenous solutions, gives injections, etc.

Joasia's mother, Ewa, still works in an office as a telephone operator. The father, Andrzej, decided several months ago to establish his own plumbing business, and is deeply in debt after investing large amounts of money to procure equipment.

What most interests us here, of course, is whether the kinetic effects associated with Joasia Gajewski are continuing even though she is past the stage of puberty. The answer is straightforward: the phenomenon persists to this day and there is no indication it will cease anytime soon. In contrast to the observations and reports from previous years, however, its manifestations are different now. For example, apart from the "flight of objects," which one eyewitness, Szymon Siedlecki, termed "common" (in the sense of being so frequent that people hardly pay attention to it anymore), totally new effects have emerged. Here we present a partial list of them.

Since February 20, 1987, water has been materializing suddenly and mysteriously in the Gajewskis' apartment. First a few drops appear on the ceiling, then practically everywhere, particularly on the walls in almost all the rooms. (We should mention there are no pipes in the places where this dripping occurs, and plumbers who come to the apartment turn off the water supply just to make sure.) Moreover, several areas "leak," causing serious damage to the furniture, such as a large couch and a sofa bed (in the latter instance the water had to be bailed out with shovels). When one of the plumbers was unable to find the source of the "leaks," he scraped off the plaster on a spot where drops had appeared. The ceiling underneath turned out to be dry!

On June 16, 1987, in addition to the "common" flight of objects, particularly eggs (which took a special liking to a wall in the hallway), there were effects straight out of science fiction. The freestanding bathtub "climbed" onto the dryer, a large picture in the parlor "hung itself" on a ceiling hook for a flower basket, glass rained down everywhere and stuck to clothing, and an ordinary colander "hissed" so loudly after flying that it seemed ready to "jump." (Unfortunately, the Gajewskis could not say whether the strainer was hot at that moment; they were afraid to come near it.)

On February 20, 1988, something Chaplinesque happened: a candle landed right in a pot of soup cooking on the stove and melted completely. Ewa Gajewski, pulling the long wick out of the pot, burst into tears—the dinner was ruined.

On March 25, 1988, Ewa and Andrzej planned to throw a party for their friends and family on Joasia's eighteenth birthday. They bought three bottles of vodka for the occasion. The next day they discovered numerous pieces of glass in one of them. The bottle caps had not been tampered with. At the time they bought the liquor—the Gajewskis are absolutely certain of this—there was no glass in the bottle.

In July 1989, at a scout camp in Jelenia Gora, various objects—forks, pans, canteens, and even towels—flew around inside the tent where Joasia slept with other girls. More serious incidents occurred as well. One scout, who reported the news that "things were flying" in the tent next to his, was beaned by hiking shoes; another boy was lashed all over his body by sandal thongs. For a while the girls were afraid to enter the tent and begged Joasia to "cut it out."

At a winter vacation center for students in Krasnystaw in 1989, all the faucets got twisted in one night (an effect similar to the ones observed earlier in the Gajewskis' apartment and at the student sanatorium in Zakopane). The resort's management ordered an investigation, which found that the "culprit" was an amiable 19-year-old schoolgirl from Czeladz near Sosnowiec.

In May 1989 a mysterious fire broke out in the Gajewskis' apartment. It happened just when Joasia, back from school, had made sandwiches and gone into the parlor. Smelling smoke, she returned to the kitchen. If anyone thinks the fire might have started there while she was making tea, we should point out that the wooden panels on the ceiling were burning. The light bulb was also shattered and its filaments glowed for a long time afterward even though the socket was broken and the electricity was turned off. The fire caused such serious damage to the panels that they had to be replaced. A subsequent inspection found the electrical system to be otherwise in good condition.

However, the most spectacular effects that have occurred since we completed our book involve the repeated, spontaneous movement of furniture in the apartment. Here is one such incident as reported by several eyewitnesses.

On the morning of October 18, 1987, Joasia called her mother at work and asked how she could get into the armoire containing her clothes. It turned out that right after Joasia had woken up, she saw the armoire "stroll" to the middle of the room, spin around, and "return" to its place—except its door was facing the wall. Equally bizarre was the behavior of a wall unit with the TV set that "marched" around the parlor. Joasia was clearly amused by these goings-on. When her frightened mother said she would come home at once, the girl replied half-jokingly: "Look for the armoire at the stop, maybe it'll pick you up."

While they were talking on the phone, the "routine" flights began—primarily tumblers and eggs, which zipped out of the closed refrigerator. Joasia rushed out to the landing, where she met Adam Imielski, a schoolboy who resided in the same building. In an interview we had with him a few days later, he described the scene:

> Joasia asked for help. She said things were flying and the furniture was "walking" too. I went into her apartment and saw glass everywhere. I also noticed an armoire moving slowly toward the middle of the room. At the same time, the doors of the wall units began slamming, and things were falling off the shelves. When I saw what was happening, I tried to save the tumblers, I didn't want them to break. Meanwhile, Joasia was standing with her back to a wall unit and picking up glass from the floor. Just then I saw the narrow middle unit lean forward and hit the back of her head. I was scared stiff, 'cause I thought it was about to crush her, but it "straightened up" and returned to its place. I can't imagine how that could've happened. Normally, if a piece of furniture tipped over that far, it would fall.

Immediately afterward, Imielski said, various objects started flying around again, this time rather aggressively. A bottle hit him in the head, raising a lump the size of a ping pong ball.

Nor did the kinetic effects occurring on that day and the following ones spare Joasia's classmate Joanna Potepa. A small kitchen knife struck her in the back, and when she was fleeing the apartment with her friend a glass "landed" on her head. The sound they heard was like the explosion of a TV tube. In our interview with Ms. Potepa, she assured us that she had no hard feelings toward Joasia; after spending lots of time with her she had grown accustomed to being the target of flying objects.

On October 21, 1987—after two days' respite—the pandemonium resumed. In Joasia's words: "I got up at quarter after seven. My parents had already left for work. The first thing I noticed was that the doors of two rooms were missing. One of them had 'slipped' out of the hinges and was leaning against the wall; the other was 'resting' against the cupboard in the dining room. Around eight o'clock things started flying. The meat grinder had 'climbed' onto the dryer again, furniture shook, and glass kept shattering on the walls. It sounded like bombs were going off."

Izabela Blechowski, a neighbor of the Gajewskis, has frequently heard the sound of "explosions" in Apt. 63. She drops in to see them occasionally but with great reluctance; she claims to feel ill once she crosses the threshold. Ms. Blechowski is frightened by the din behind the wall, and often has the impression that the whole building is about to collapse around her: "I break out in a cold sweat, I'm afraid to live here at all. I constantly hear noises as if the walls were crumbling. Even now, as I talk to you, it's hard for me to concentrate. I have to live too, I've got small children."

Finally, we should note that unlike the initial period of Joasia's internship at the hospital, while she was in her freshman and sophomore years at the nursing school, the kinetic effects have not occurred.

During our last visit to Czeladz, on October 14, 1989, in the company of Mr. Joel Stern, a translator from the United States, and Dr. Maciej Kociecki, a professor at the Warsaw Polytechnic Institute, Joasia bent two spoons at our request. (She accomplished this by rubbing them, the first for a considerable length of time, the second for only a few minutes.) She also answered a number of questions pertaining more to her personal attitude than to the physical aspects of the phenomenon, which, we believe, have already been described in sufficient detail. Here are some of the questions we asked:

Q. After six years, how do you feel about the phenomena you must still deal with?
A. I accept them now; I'm used to the situation.

Q. Do they frighten you?

A. No, they sort of amuse me.

Q. Have you ever tried to find a rational explanation for all this?

A. I don't think I'll ever think up anything on my own, when people smarter than me have failed. Nor do I want any publicity—why should I? If this has to happen, I've got to know how to live with it.

Q. Do you remember your dreams?

A. Very seldom. I usually forget them right after I wake up. If I do remember one, it means something is about to happen.

Q. Do you want to work as a nurse in a hospital when you finish school?

A. Yes, except I'd like to take a two-year postgraduate medical course before then.

Q. Do you think this is a suitable profession for you?

A. Contact with sick people suits me. I want to help them.

2015

The psychokinetic phenomena surrounding Joasia Gajewski, which were most intense in 1983-1985, eventually began to taper off toward the end of her adolescence. After graduating from nursing school, Joasia found work in her chosen vocation, then married, changed her name, and had two children. She also moved from the place where she had lived since childhood. For a while she kept in touch sporadically with Dr. Eustachiusz Gadula, but this contact broke off too.

Regrettably, we have not been able to discover Joasia's new whereabouts, especially as her parents have passed away in the interim. We might add that finding someone with a possibly changed surname in the urban agglomeration of Polish Silesia, with its multi-million population, is a nearly insurmountable task. A direct appeal we made to Joasia in our monthly magazine *Nieznany Świat* [*The Unknown World*], which seeks to analyze paranormal phenomena, unexplained events from the past, and the mysteries of Nature, likewise proved unsuccessful. Hoping to get an update regarding her life today and her perspective on the events of bygone years, this appeal, printed in the September edition, failed to elicit a response either from Joasia herself or from someone with knowledge of her subsequent fate.

And so, the psychokinetic powers of the teenager from Sosnowiec remain a mystery to this day.

Appendix 1
Hypotheses

From the very outset, statements on the Joasia Gajewski phenomenon, especially articles in the press, have put forward more or less sensational hypotheses about it. Some of them are clearly mistaken, while others, albeit flawed, offer interesting and thought-provoking interpretations. With the help of Dr. Eustachiusz Gadula and our personal files, we have assembled a number of these hypotheses and explanations. In presenting them we make no effort to judge their validity.

From Biogravitation to.........Frustration

Biogravitational powers. Proponents of this hypothesis argue that the phenomena associated with Joasia Gajewski occur with particular frequency among adolescent girls. They speak of biological particles and emission of gravitational waves constituting gravitational fields. Some authors believe psychokinetic phenomena are triggered by the biogravitational field emitted by specialized brain cells.

This concept was developed most fully by Adam Wojciechowski in *Przegląd Tygodniowy* (no. 25/83):

"Just as the sun attracts the Earth, and the Earth the moon, so biological particles also attract one another. They are linked by the force of biogravitation. The combination of such forces gives rise to a biogravitational field. We had not been aware of this because — as eminent Soviet physicist Pyotr Kapitsa has found — it is only when elementary particles occur in large aggregates that the forces we call gravitation begin to play a role among them. In describing the quantum and electrical interaction of atoms, the characteristics of gravitation are not taken into account, for it is manifested in nature only in large masses.

"But since every vibrating particle is capable of emitting gravitational waves, these in turn can form a gravitational field. And the biogravitational field produced by specialized centers in the brain can penetrate any barrier irrespective of distance, set objects in motion, be transformed into various kinds of energy, accelerate the sedimentation processes of colloidal solutions, light up semiconductor crystals, expose camera film at a distance, etc.

"The theory of the existence of a biogravitational field produced by living organisms makes it necessary to reexamine the previous assumptions of quantum physics. Models describing the behavior of elementary particles have always been approximate, incomplete, and imperfect.

"The indeterminacy principle has recognized the limitations of our knowledge. Only those fields and interrelations through which we come to know the world and the statistical behavior of its basic constituents and particles can be real. We experience events indirectly, through the prism of subjective perception. Hence, if what we experience is merely a function of our mind and not the objective truth, our knowledge remains limited."

Biomagnetic energy. According to this hypothesis, which is based on the findings of Russian researchers, bioenergetic forces are activated in girls during puberty. Changes occurring in the body's cells produce a bioenergetic field, whose energy source is the splitting of chromosomes. Because the field arises in a "wet" medium, its effect is particularly strong. After puberty these forces generally disappear.

Radiation of the primary field. Some scientists maintain that all known fields (i.e., electrical, magnetic, electromagnetic, gravitational, and so on) derive from a primary field. "Its existence is proved by the sudden alterations in the frequency of an electromagnetic field. The primary field has not yet been defined, but we can assume it is vitally important for life." (Cited from a statement by physicist Jerzy Sosnowski for the weekly magazine *Polityka*, no. 25, 1983.)

Peculiar connections between various types of fields (especially electromagnetic and electrostatic). See the interview with Dr. Andrzej Franek in the chapter "Comprehensive Studies."

Gravitational resonance. A hypothesis postulating that living organisms generate a gravitational resonance that neutralizes the gravitational field. Such resonance may arise from a particular diet (an excess of certain elements in the body) or from "incessant infrasounds," i.e., so-called centers of excitation (perhaps new, artificial ones to which man has not yet adapted or which "he cannot not even conceive of").

A state of collective hypnosis (hallucination). Persons describing phenomena of one kind or another are convinced they really saw them, while actually they were in a hypnotic or hallucinatory state. But this would still not explain who or what could have caused the physical effects.

Etheric energy. A hypothesis put forward by psychics who believe there is no point at all in studying the matter, since Joasia Gajewski is simply a marvelous channel able to establish contact, even unconsciously, with the astral plane.

A mere hoax. An explanation just as plausible as the others. No comment.

Twilight of the Paradigms
An Interview with Professor Arkadiusz Goral

Professor Arkadiusz Goral is a prominent specialist in the field of solid-state electronics. Born in Siedlice in 1930, he majored in electrical engineering at the Szczecin Polytechnic Institute and continued his studies at the Military Technical Academy. He received two doctorates in 1961 and 1963 respectively at the Warsaw Polytechnic Institute, and in 1970 attained the rank of professor. He was co-winner of the State Prize in 1964 for designing the production of ferrites; served in 1955-1968 as director of the Subassemblies Plant at the Military Institute of Communications and concurrently in 1965-1969 as director of the Microelectronics Plant at the Institute of Telecommunications and Radio Engineering. In 1958-1964 he lectured on metallurgy and magnetic subassemblies in the Department of Electronics at the Warsaw Institute of Technology. Four years later he became head of the Department of Electronic and Microelectronic Technology at the WIT.

Professor Goral initiated and in 1967-1972 directed the national development program of hybrid microelectronics. In 1969-1971 he organized the Scientific Production Center, serving as its director. In 1963-1972 Professor Goral served as chairman of the microelectronics problem-solving team of the Main Electronics and Telecommunication Commission under the Science and Technology Committee. At the same time, he dealt with issues relating to the reliability of subassemblies and electronic equipment within the framework of the coordination activities of the Polish Academy of Sciences.

Professor Goral's scientific interests span the entire field of electronics. He has published over 130 papers in numerous Polish and foreign journals and participated in more than a dozen international conferences. Among the books he has authored or co-authored, one (*Nonparametric Magnetic Amplifiers*) represents an original contribution to the theory of nonlinear magnetic circuits; another, *Technika warsztatowa w mikroelektronice* (*Workshop Technology in Microelectronics*), outlines a national R&D program for hybrid microelectronics. Professor Goral is also the co-founder and president of the Polish Synergy Association.

Q. In a series of articles you wrote for the journal *Przeglad Techniczny* in 1982-1985, and above all in your book *Meandry fizyki* [*The Circuitous Path of Physics*], you challenge and rebel against the physics paradigm. Even those who declare themselves your opponents concede that the theories you advance (concerning the dual nature of the electron, for example) are thought-provoking and valuable from a scientific point of view. Without going into an exhaustive discussion here, we'd like to ask if we should conclude from your arguments that the model of physics based largely on Einstein's theory of relativity and long considered unshakeable is now beginning to prove inadequate for understanding and interpreting the phenomena that physicists must deal with today.

A. The matter isn't that simple. In regard to the problem at hand—gravitational anomalies—as early as 1921 Erwin Schrodinger, the co-originator of quantum mechanics, pointed out that in certain frames of reference energy and the momentum of the gravitational field of Einstein-Hilbert equations disappear beyond the region of the gravity source.

Q. How is that important?

A. It's extremely important. Einstein strongly emphasized that the electromagnetic field is a material entity to which one can attribute mass, whereas Maxwell introduced the concept of field momentum. Einstein's response to Schrodinger's caveats is quite characteristic. Einstein declared he could see no reason why the gravitational field should behave like an electromagnetic field.

Q. How do scientists look upon the matter today, more than sixty years after that discussion?

A. The Russian professor Logunov and his colleagues commented on this problem in 1979. His actual words were: "If the theory (i.e., the general theory of relativity) reduces the energy and momentum of a field to zero, it would mean that physical effects can be generated at a distance by spiritual forces. Hence, such a theory does not belong in physics." In the same work, Logunov proposed a theory based on nonlinear geometry in which the energy and momentum of a field are not reduced to zero in any frame of reference.

Q. Does that resolve the whole problem?

A. Yes, according to the "orderly" geometry of time and space, which has no internal contradictions. Incidentally, Logunov, Mereshvili, and their colleagues did not stop there. In January 1986, they published a work in which they showed that equivalence between the gravitational and the inertial mass is only a particular case in the general theory of relativity.

Q. ???

A. Your surprise is justified, since children are taught in school that the two masses are equal, and this remains a mandatory paradigm. Professor Logunov, however, doubts it for another reason. He simply cannot understand how the inequality of those masses from the viewpoint of the general theory of relativity could have been overlooked for so many years.

Q. Excuse us, could you please explain for the benefit of readers who are not conversant with physics: what exactly are inertial and gravitational masses?

A. All right, let's start with inertial mass. It constitutes the measure of energy in a physical body. It's simply a different representation of this energy. If we multiply the mass by a constant factor equal to the speed of light squared, we receive the formula $E=mc^2$, universally recognized with Einstein's theory of special relativity.

Q. Is the formula really valid?

A. Einstein himself demonstrated in a 1947 paper (he repeated this conclusion in the book *Out of My Later Years*) that the formula $E=mc^2$ is directly derived from Maxwell's theory and the principle of conservation of energy. Einstein was never too concerned about his fellow physicists' opinions, whether they were critical or laudatory. That is yet another hallmark of his greatness.

Q. What about gravitational mass?

A. It's proportional to the force of gravitational attraction. Let's say the mass of the Earth is "M," while "m" stands for our own mass. If we now multiply these two values by the constant of gravity and then divide the square of the distance from the center of the Earth, we'll obtain the force of gravity.

Q. But that was discovered by Newton.

A. Of course, except that the paradigm of the equivalence between the two masses—gravitational and inertial—was incorporated into the general theory of relativity. Unjustifiably, it turns out.

Q. How is all this connected with the kinetic phenomena occurring around Joasia Gajewski?

A. We'll get to that shortly. First let me conclude my argument. Now, since we are speaking of gravitational mass, the question naturally arises: What is the gravitational mass of an elementary particle? Let's take the example of the "heavy lepton," the so-called tau particle (tauon) discovered in 1976. It has an energy of 1785 MeV, nearly twice that of a proton (938 MeV). However, the tauon doesn't live longer than one picosecond (ten-trillionths of a second). That's a long lifespan for an elementary particle, but in the meantime the Earth's gravitational field may not even "discover" that an accelerator-generated tauon exists. Of course, I'm using "discover" figuratively, since the Earth's gravitational field has no consciousness. Consciousness is replaced here by definite physical effects. It's difficult to speak of physical effects, though; during its "life" the tauon emits electromagnetic radiation for a distance of a few millimeters. Then the particle disappears, leaving only the products of its disintegration. To this day we still don't know how much these products weigh. Likewise, the neutrino, which probably has a rest mass equal to zero, does not enter into gravitation.

In short, there's still no theory of gravitation on the subatomic level. To put it more precisely, we don't know the inner physical mechanism of gravitational forces.

Q. What about quantum physics? Doesn't it deal primarily with subatomic processes?

A. Please! In quantum physics, electrons (as well as muons and tauons) have no internal structure. They are points with infinite energy and an infinite charge. The observable mass and electrical charge are brought into the theory from without and are conceived as the difference between two infinities. From the viewpoint of quantum electrodynamics, it therefore doesn't matter whether the electron has the mass we assume or whether it weighs ten tons!

Q. What about the efforts to develop a unified-field theory that are attracting so much attention?

A. Those efforts aim at standardizing or rather formalizing the description of the four basic interactions occurring in nature: gravitational, electromagnetic, weak, and strong. The first two are long-distance and limited to the vicinity of elementary particles.

But I wonder, what's the sense of unifying something without try-ing to understand the physical mechanism of the interactions? And what can we unify at all, given the incredible conceptual confusion prevailing in physics at the present time?

Q. Does that apply to the main topic of our conversation?

A. Absolutely. Let me give you one more example: the lepton, known as the muon (previously "meson"). This particle has been studied thoroughly, and it's used in medical radiology, among other areas. We know that its life rest mass is approximately 1.5 microseconds. A muon accelerated to a velocity comparable to the speed of light lives much longer, and this fact is presented as evidence for the so-called dilation of time resulting from the special theory of relativity. Nonetheless, quantum physics stub-bornly teaches that even an electron must not be treated on the microscale as a loaded bullet. On the one hand, an electron (like the muon) has the characteristics of a point: on the other, it's en-veloped in a cloud of probabilities described by the famous func-tion "psi." Even from the classical point of view, a muon acceler-ated to a velocity close to the speed of light represents a totally different quality. In both quantum and classical physics, it will be a bundle of waves with an energy far exceeding the rest energy of the muon. The bundle disperses and interacts with other particles long after the muon "dies." While this is an undeniable fact, it would be hard to use it as a justification for the dilation of time in the system of coordinates of a moving muon "bullet." Physicists seem unconcerned about this, and they have yet to investigate (by means of a specific program) the numerical connection between the charge of an electron and Planck's constant. Professor Martin Perl (the head of the research team that discovered the tauon) leaves this problem for future generations of "brighter" physicists to solve.

Q. We learned from our conversations with the staff at the Warsaw School of Engineering that you proposed a solution to the problem…

A. Yes, eight years ago, within the framework of an electro-magnetic theory. But scientists abroad don't read the *Foreign Bul-letin of the PAN* [Polish Academy of Sciences], and our physicists label such attempts "parascience." A certain well-known physi-cist-poet did that a few years ago.

Q. Let's dot the "i" then: can gravitation be linked to mass and energy?

A. Under terrestrial conditions, yes, because what exists here consists of electrons, protons, and neutrons, which are stable par-ticles. To be sure, the neutron lives only about a thousandth of a second and therefore doesn't have the stability of a free particle, but in the nuclear core it's a stable particle in combination with the proton. Thus, with respect to terrestrial conditions and stable particles, the inertial and gravitational masses are in fact equal. But we don't know if this holds true for the universe as a whole, because our knowledge is quite limited in this regard.

Q. Gravitational waves haven't been detected yet...

A. Exactly. They seem to be inherent in Einstein's theory, but attempts to detect them have failed. We don't even know if those waves are transverse or longitudinal. Since we know nothing about them, it's very difficult to devise experiments confirming their existence. Now, someone said on TV not long ago that our failure to detect gravitational waves basically confirms Einstein's theory, because they are so weak as to be undetectable. That kind of reasoning won't get us very far.

Q. Then which path should we take?

A. You're asking me a question which the greatest physicists in the world have been pondering for years. The problem of gravi-tation was studied even by Maxwell, who theorized in one of his works that the gravitational field has tremendous energy, surpass-ing all known electrical or magnetic fields. If we tried to explain gravitational force through an analysis of this energy, deducing it in the form of an equation by analogy to a magnetic field, we would probably arrive at conclusions incompatible with our pres-ent concepts. That's precisely why Maxwell stopped short of his goal. He literally said: "I cannot go this way."

Q. But in your theory on the dual nature of the electron you refer to Maxwell's equations.

A. Yes, because Maxwell's contributions are indisputable. Six years ago, I hit upon the idea of using data from my own model alone to calculate the ratio between the masses of the proton and neutron. And so...

Q. Professor, we see you're about to write some mathematical formulas on the blackboard. Couldn't you just describe your concept to us?

A. All right. I wanted to find a general theoretical basis for the whole model, which I might express as follows: The gravitational field "doesn't know" what energy its individual particles contain. It simply has some kind of structure plus processes that it reacts to. Thus, there must be something that creates this field. I assumed that the factor producing the Maxwellian electromagnetic field is the interior of my hypothetical structure and what we call the degree of rotational freedom. The gravitational field, on the other hand, is connected with translatory motion occurring along a radius. According to this concept, gravitational waves would be longitudinal, like sound waves dispersing in the air.

The basic problem here is, what shall we take as the measure of the gravitational charge? By analogy to the electrical or magnetic charge, I assumed that the *gravitational charge is connected with the particle's subtle structure* (not with the mass itself, which the field "knows nothing about"). As the measure of the gravitational charge, I used an energy "integral"—not energy but an integral of energy, for if we assume that a stream of energy is radiating, the charge must have a higher, integrated nature. This likewise holds true for an electric charge and the electric current derived from it.

Of course, I assume here that the energies are in equilibrium. In other words, the stream of energy arising from the universal gravitational field counterbalances the stream of energy flowing from our particle. When a balance exists, the particle is stable.

The crux of my argument is this: *if it's true that the gravitational charge accumulates in the particle's outer envelope (which I designate as "subtle"), it may therefore be possible to affect this particle and change its gravitational field without greatly disturbing its energy.* The entire phenomenon, I repeat, is connected with the particle's structure, and there's no need at all to change its energy to any significant extent. It was on this basis that I calculated a gravitational charge for the proton and electron. I obtained the figure 1835.9, which is close to the experimental ratio of the masses: 1836.15.

Bearing in mind that the more than satisfactory agreement between my theory and this figure might be coincidental, I then checked the suitability of my model for calculating the lepton spectrum. The model proved to be accurate: taking the existence of the electron as a starting point, I succeeded in calculating the masses of the next leptons—the muon and tauon.

Q. We know that already!

A. Yes, but not the masses of the following leptons in the spectrum, which I can also predict. To be specific, the next lepton should have a mass (energy) of approximately 27 GeV, and the one after that–430 GeV. I won't mention the higher leptons, for their tremendous energies would mean little to the readers.

Q. In other words, you think that you've predicted what physicists may discover in the future?

A. They may, but it's not certain they will. There's no need for experimental verification of this model. It's already been verified in the case of the so-called standard model, which most physicists "believe in" (that's the very expression they use). Studies with accelerators are an incredibly expensive proposition. If I had the funds at my disposal, however, I wouldn't hesitate to finance such a research project.

Q. And what results would you expect?

A. I'm convinced the lepton spectrum is infinite. Discovery of my super tau lepton with an energy of 27 GeV would make "quarkologists" multiply the number of quarks. We'd no longer be compelled to lump together leptons and quarks simply because they share a few extrinsic features. Wonderful new vistas would open up.

Q. Getting back to the subject that brought us here, how is all this important for comprehending the Joasia Gajewski phenomenon?

A. We must remember that what we call the gravitational field, which is observable only under terrestrial conditions, is not the gravitational field prevailing throughout the universe. Its energy represents an infinitesimal fraction of that field. It's a disturbance, a sort of anomaly, which we live in but are generally unaware of because gravitational energy is negligible, the least of all known forms of energy.

If we look at the functioning of the living organism in this context, hundreds of questions immediately arise. We still know little, after all, about the physical structure of living organisms. Physics, chemistry, and biophysics are unable to answer fundamental questions in this area. For example, they can't explain such an elementary thing as the characteristics of intercellular membranes and passage between them. Yet the intercellular membrane, which is a micron thick and has millivolt potentials, can accumulate an electrical field of kilovolts per meter!

It thus seems very likely (or any rate, not impossible) that a certain configuration of fields, even electromagnetic ones, may disturb the gravitational field to such an extent as to generate definite physical effects like unusually strong attraction or repulsion. This is presumably what we're dealing with in Joasia Gajewski's case.

Q. So you think a local disturbance of the gravitational field is involved?

A. More than that—a local disturbance of elementary forces, because the energies of the field we use are negligible compared with other forms of energy in nature that may cause a local disturbance of the gravitational field.

Q. Do you believe the girl's entire body generates disturbances of elementary forces?

A. I suspect that her brain plays a major role. Neurophysiology would undoubtedly be helpful in explaining the phenomenon. Unfortunately, neurophysiologists aren't eager to collaborate in this area. I myself once proposed such collaboration, but it never went beyond good intentions. There are neurophysiologists interested in such questions, but officially they refuse to have anything to do with them for fear of criticism from their superiors.

Q. Is it your opinion that the hypothesis of local disturbances of elementary forces accounts for the phenomena occurring around the girl?

A. Absolutely. Let's take a look at the bent spoons you brought along. The forces "binding" the metal together were locally disrupted; they were quite weak to begin with. They seem powerful to us because it's very hard to bend a spoon by rubbing, and the great majority of people would be unable to achieve such an effect. But compared to the other forces in nature, they're a mere trifle. If my hypothesis regarding the concentration of gravitational force in the particle's subtle envelope is correct (and I'm positive it is), it may be possible to disturb the equilibrium of this envelope and switch the direction of the energy flow. This could affect the universal field in such a way as to transform attraction into repulsion, for example. The mechanism of the phenomenon seems perfectly obvious, even though we can't explain it. And so, just as Maxwell was baffled by the Earth's gravitational field, we have our own mysteries too. For instance, we don't know how to "reconcile" the Earth's gravitational field with what I shall term the biogravitational field. It's an important question, for if we assume that the mechanism of biogravitation causes elementary disturbances, we must agree that abnormal movement of objects also disrupts transmission of electromagnetic radiation. In other words, what we see and hear is partly an "illusion" since our senses and ability to perceive are also changed the moment the field is disturbed. Moreover, the energy causing the spontaneous movement is much greater than we think.

Q. Why?

A. Because at the critical moment the gravitational field probably releases far more energy than the girl herself was emitting. Its mechanism can be likened to the trigger of a rifle: a light squeeze is sufficient to produce violent effects. The same is true of lightning.

In general, I suspect that what we are dealing with here isn't energy but solely conservation of action. In quantum theory, where concentration of energy may be violated in accordance with the Heisenberg Principle, this is a rather simple thing. Thus, if Joasia Gajewski causes some sort of elementary action, a disturbance of fundamental forces, the energy involved must be enormous.

Q. Does that mean there is no chance of consciously controlling the phenomenon?

A. The girl can't control it because the state of excitation affects her as well as the matter around her. Is there any possibility of controlling it in the future? I think if neurologists did a
serious study of the whole problem, we'd probably be able to at
least predict inner states of excitation, which would enable us—
indirectly—to control other phenomena as well. The problem is
formidable, and we have no idea how to begin tackling it. Should
we use pharmacology? Definite fields? Nobody knows.

Q. We've provided you with an exact description of the
acoustical effects we witnessed and that often (though not always)
precede the movement of objects around Joasia Gajewski. How is
one to explain them?

A. If we assume that spontaneous movement of objects contrary to the known laws of physics is a reality (and in light of the
evidence you presented—numerous eyewitness accounts plus
similar observations under laboratory conditions—there seems
to be no doubt about it), air particles must also go into motion,
thereby generating acoustical waves. It's therefore quite likely that
the air will start to vibrate before actual effects occur. You'll then
hear crackling, rustling, droning, whistling, and so on, because all
this has the same physical basis: simply the constant disturbance
of the subtle envelope of elementary particles.

Q. Let's consider another kinetic effect that has often been
observed: the passage of objects through walls. For a long time,
we were hesitant to include this in our report, but we decided
there was no point in keeping the matter hushed up. There are
many indications the phenomenon really exists, incredible as it
seems.

A. Well, if we grant that the Joasia Gajewski phenomenon is
contrary to the known laws of physics under conditions of terrestrial gravitation, we might as well accept the fact that objects can
pass through walls. What exactly is "passage?" It's one of the possible effects of the absence or weakening of normal interactions.
According to one plausible hypothesis, for example, parallel to
us, in the same dimension of time and space, there are N entities;

but because no interactions take place between them, they will remain "unaware" of each other. This assumption seems scientifically well-founded and valid to me. On the other hand, take the theory of quarks. Though quarks have never been detected, this hasn't kept people from theorizing about them. Therefore, we've accepted the concept of the existence of hypothetical entities. From this point of view, one can say that the theory of quarks makes much less sense than the notion of objects passing through solid matter: no one has ever found quarks, but passage (if one is to believe the eyewitness accounts) has been observed.

Since we assume Joasia Gajewski causes suspension of normal interactions, she could just as easily disrupt them, for these interactions serve to link atoms together. Such passage might occur then—why not?

Q. The observers say the objects are destroyed or deformed after going through walls…

A. Of course. Since the objects are affected by forces that disrupt atomic bonds, it's no wonder they look the way they do. It's hard to believe the girl could have generated uniform fields facilitating "smooth" passage.

Q. What about changes in temperature? The eyewitnesses claim that objects felt warm after flying through the air, and that this warmth soon disappeared.

A. It all depends on the mechanism of the local change of elementary interactions. If a great amount of energy is liberated during a disturbance, an object may even melt. But this needn't happen, as we are generally dealing here with non-thermal processes. Let me reemphasize—the key factor here is disruption of atomic bonds and weakening of the existing structure.

Q. What do you think, Professor Goral: Will physics be able in the foreseeable future to explain such cases as the Sosnowiec phenomenon on the basis of a universally recognized theory?

A. I'm extremely pessimistic on that score. Physics hasn't been able yet to resolve the inner contradictions in theories accepted by the majority of physicists. The relativist void is being populated with made up entities. Lately quarks themselves have already become "too big," and there's an ongoing search for still tinier elementary particles, which are called "preons" and other fanciful terms. For some, this is a diverting mathematical pursuit.

Unfortunately, extreme intolerance and dogmatism have been rife in physics for decades. Most physicists create a world of their own and are not bothered even by stern reprimands coming from eminent colleagues such as Dirac now or Heisenberg in the past. Polish physicists can be particularly egregious in this regard. One of our luminaries, for example, criticized Heisenberg for undermining the conceptual validity of quarks, although that same luminary simply misinterpreted the arguments he set forth in *Was ist ein Elementarteilchen?* [*What is an Elementary Particle?*].

Getting back to the question you just posed, I would respond this way: To me, it's more likely that priestly celibacy will be abolished in the Roman Catholic Church before a major paradigm shift takes place in physics.

Elusive Waves
An Interview with Engineer Grzegorz Zapalski

Mr. Grzegorz Zapalski is an electrical engineer at the Nuclear Research Institute in Krakow. He graduated from the School of Communications at the Warsaw Polytechnic Institute. For thirty years he has been engaged in constructing equipment used in nuclear physics as well as detectors for measuring weak physical fields. He is a member of the team appointed by the Ministry of Health and Social Welfare to study the Joasia Gajewski phenomenon. In consenting to the publication of this interview, he cautioned that the views expressed in it were his alone and should not be attributed to the scientific institution where he works.

Q. It's clear from our discussions that you believe the kinetic effects occurring around Joasia Gajewski are due to gravitational waves, or rather gravitational disturbances.

A. Exactly. In a collection of scientific essays (*Classical and Nuclear Physics*, published in Moscow in 1974 and translated into Polish in 1978), Russian physicists Vladimir L. Braginsky and Valentin N. Rudenko state that gravitational waves, like magnetic waves, are nothing but a labile gravitational field existing apart from sources and dispersing freely in space. Assuming this is true, gravitational waves should affect—by means of specific forces—the masses encountered in their path, while the bodies within their range undergo acceleration. Of course, these need not be the sine curve waveforms universally present in nature; they could even be individual impulses appearing quite randomly.

Gravitational waves come to us from space. They originate in (among other things) binary stars revolving around a common center of gravity. Because the stream of these waves is uniform (in view of the dimensions of the universe), they have an equal and simultaneous effect on our body and, say, a table in the room. That's why we don't notice them in our environment. Besides, the energy they produce is very slight.

Many theoretical works have been written about gravitational waves and the mechanisms producing them. Still, we don't know how these waves arise in living organisms. There are only hypotheses. In Joasia Gajewski's case, it seems we are dealing with a living generator that operates spontaneously, randomly, and over a limited area. It's precisely for this reason Joasia (unlike waves from outer space) affects only certain objects but with relatively great energy. One result of the functioning of this peculiar, living generator is local curvature of space.

Q. What does that mean?

A. To put it as simply as possible, every mass disrupts space as though bending the spatial axes. That's what Einstein claims, and this theory has been verified on a universal scale by the diffraction of starlight when passing through the gravitational field of the sun, for example. This curvature of space, or rather the constant gravitational field produced by mass, is manifested as acceleration.

We are familiar with terrestrial acceleration and feel it from birth to the moment of death. But since (according to Einstein) gravitational waves also affect mass as acceleration, it is conceivable that these waves, with a suitably large amount of energy, could bend space completely into some sort of loop. Such effects on a universal scale might be expected in black holes, but that's a different problem altogether.

Q. In your opinion, then, this curvature of space would account for such phenomena as telekinesis, clairvoyance, and teleportation?

A. It's highly probable, especially if it turns out that gravitational waves or disturbances disperse more quickly than light in a vacuum or travel at an infinite speed (which is not out of the question). The speed of light has been measured quite precisely and by many methods, whereas we can only hypothesize about the speed of gravitational dispersion in the context of theoretical cases. The phenomenon of clairvoyance, for example, can be imagined as a certain form of gravitational holography. Thus, a clairvoyant would "attune" his own brain waves to the remnant of the gravitational image in some object (belonging to a lost person, for instance) and emit his waves into space in various directions. After hitting upon the lost person or his gravitational trace, the wave would return the desired information.

Perhaps dowsers "attune" themselves to water or minerals in a similar fashion. The radiesthetic sense cannot be attributed to any electrical, magnetic, or electromagnetic forces. All such explanations seem simplistic. Of course, there may be other forces unknown to science, except in that case we would be talking about magic rather than physics.

But let's go back to gravitation. If we managed to generate a sufficiently powerful wave in a specific area, it could possibly bend the coordinates in such a manner as to move this area to another space.

Q. How can that be proved?

A. Well, it's just a hypothesis that cannot be proved at our present stage of knowledge, although theoretical works on the subject already exist. Popular science literature has the concept of "flatlings," two-dimensional creatures living on a specific plane. On a different, parallel plane, there are other "flatlings." Communication between them is impossible because there's no connection. However, if those surfaces were to become warped for some reason, even in a tiny segment, they could meet one another and a "flatling" might be able to pass into another space.

Obviously we needn't take this notion seriously. But if the model of reasoning on which it's based were extrapolated to our world, one could assume that apart from the three known dimensions a kind of "superspace" exists, whereby it would be possible to pass into a different space when the one we are living in gets warped.

Q. Isn't that sheer fantasy?

A. Not necessarily. The latest hypotheses on the Big Bang, the zero moment when time did not yet exist and matter was inconceivably dense, postulate that an infinite number of spaces arose then, and that they can't communicate with one another unless they are bent.

Of course, I don't assume that every person who has paranormal abilities can cause such tremendous disruptions of space whenever he wants. Many psychic phenomena (such as mental ones that occur without kinetic effects—dowsing, telepathy, or teledetection) utilize rather small gravitational disturbances in which the waves are of very low intensity.

Q. If we've understood you correctly, the source of gravitational waves is the human brain?

A. Not quite. Several sources have been found in the human body, such as the pituitary gland, the pancreas, and the fingertips (this last source is used, for example, in bending spoons through rubbing or in biotherapy). I personally believe, however, that life itself in its broadest sense is based on gravitation, specifically biogravitation on the molecular level. Obviously life would be affected to a crucial extent by gravitational waves of a definite frequency or even phase characteristic of the given organism. As one example, we can cite biotherapeutic treatment to strengthen a patient's bioenergy field, which, after all, is not a constant. This hypothesis, which is increasingly gaining acceptance in the world, is very problematic, but it seems to offer the best and fullest explanation for paranormal phenomena that have been recorded and conclusively proved.

Q. Professor Wlodzimierz Sedlak maintains that life is light. What do you think of this notion?

A. I don't agree with his hypothesis for several reasons. By "light" Professor Sedlak means electromagnetic waves. It's true we live in a huge "electromagnetic dump" of which we are unaware. Our bodies are constantly penetrated by millions of various radio waves and many diverse magnetic and electrical fields emitted by devices we use every day. These fields and waves are often much stronger than those produced by human cells, yet they don't change our own vibrations or waves. Thus, if life were electromagnetic in nature as Professor Sedlak claims, it would have disappeared from Earth long ago.

The other aspect of the problem is kinetic action (as in Joasia Gajewski's case). Let's pose a question: How much energy would the girl's body have to produce in order to propel a glass against a wall? Anyone who remembers a little about electrostatics from school understands that a potential of millions of volts would be needed, which Joasia could never generate. Her measured potentials are low. But they may create a secondary effect, like ionization of the milieu by gravitational waves. The same holds true for magnetic fields, which when sufficiently strong may set a key or other piece of iron in motion, but definitely not non-magnetic objects.

Q. So the brain isn't important here?

A. I'm not saying that. It's estimated the human brain, its metabolism, generates ten to twenty watts. Let's suppose that only ten percent of this power, or one to two watts, can be radiated in the form of a gravitational impulse or gravitational wave; then let's compare this ratio with a radio wave. Now, if you have a 1-watt transmitter and a directional antenna, you can communicate over a distance of hundreds and even thousands of miles, though radio waves become attenuated when they travel through space! Telepathy and other phenomena of this kind, however, basically cannot be blocked (as we can see from telepathy experiments conducted with persons aboard submarines).

Q. But the existence of gravitational waves hasn't been experimentally verified...

A. The problem is to detect them, and for that we need to build a device that would convert gravitational waves as faithfully as possible (which means not altering their frequency) into a form of energy we know, such as an electric current, which we could then amplify and record. Attempts to detect them—by means of direct action on a concentrated mass (for example, metal cylinders weighing several tons that have converters of vibrations into electrical current)—are underway in at least a dozen scientific centers throughout the world. Increasingly sensitive devices are being constructed for this purpose; by cooling a cylindrical antenna to the temperature of liquid helium, for instance, a dramatic increase in sensitivity can be gained. Studies are also being conducted on the simultaneity of signals obtained from detectors hundreds and even thousands of miles apart in order to rule out seismic influences. In their work, Rudenko and Braginski describe projects for other, much more sensitive detectors that would operate on the same principle yet enable us to record high and low frequency waves.

But this still doesn't seem to be the solution we are after. There are undoubtedly certain interconnections between electromagnetism and gravitation that would make it possible to detect or generate gravitational waves with far more efficiency than the ordinary rotary motion of two identical masses around a common center of gravity. Such a formula will surely be found some day (recently there have been a spate of theoretical studies on this subject), and the person who discovers it will win the Nobel Prize. What will happen then to our concept of the world and reality is hard to predict at this time.

Q. What bearing does all this have on the Joasia Gajewski phenomenon?

A Joasia must be generating local disturbances of the Earth's gravitational field, or else directed gravitational waves. That would account for the kinetic effects and other phenomena.

Q. Do you believe the mystery can be solved by means of the existing research tools in physics?

A. No, for they measure only the secondary effects of gravitational radiation (like the increase in potential resulting from ionization) but not the gravitational wave itself. To find the key to the phenomenon, we would need a new principle of detection and a type of detector based on it (e.g., a device for measuring the curvature of space in a small area, say, a square centimeter). In the development of such a device, Joasia could play a useful role as generator of a non-uniform gravitational wave.

Peculiar Cell Metabolism
A Conversation with Professor Lech Jan Radwanowski

Lech Jan Radwanowski is an architect and a specialist in biocenotics. He received his professional training at the Warsaw Polytechnic Institute and the Silesian Polytechnic Institute. For many years he has been active as a lecturer and author in Poland and abroad. Professor Radwanowski's primary interests are environmental design and engineering in accordance with biocenotic principles, and research on the characteristics of underground waters. The crowning achievement of his scientific endeavors is his GeoMHD theory on the radiation of watercourses. According to this theory, such radiation represents a very complex type of geomagnetic-hydrodynamic vibration consisting of electromagnetic (photon) waves, acoustical (sonic) waves, and so-called Alfven waves.

Lech J. Radwanowski was the co-founder and president (in 1983-1984) of the now defunct Polish Biocenotic Association. He is regarded as furthering Professor Stefan Manczarski's research on so-called non-static phenomena (biotronics).

Q. When the psychokinetic phenomena associated with Joasia Gajewski began occurring in April 1983, you were one of the first to conduct tests and experiments with the girl. What's your general hypothesis on the origin of these phenomena?

A. Before I address that question, a few words of explanation are in order. Now, we are always bandying about the term "paranormal phenomena," which I really don't find appropriate, since it implies a lack of philosophical or scientific concepts for defining the subject of a study. The expression "metaphysical phenomena" that is sometimes used is even less suitable, for current interpretations of the universe concern the metamorphic phase of a mesomorphic state. All this imprecision reflects the helplessness of science in regard to the phenomena it must deal with.

I believe science is an activity in which there is no place for any "para." But it can accommodate concepts based on observed phenomena, which cannot be random because this would contradict the laws of probability. And I don't think there's any reason not to accept these laws in the context of the problems under discussion.

I've been studying biotronic phenomena for thirty years, since 1956. From the outset I believed that radiesthetic perception was a reality and could be used to assess environmental influences on health. Unfortunately, I wasn't able to achieve my goals, mainly because of a lack of understanding for problems of this kind. Electrochemistry, electrophysiology, and biophysics in the true sense of the word did not exist then. Also, such researchers as Wiktor Bernacki, Stefan Manczarski, Julian Aleksandrowicz, Wlodzimierz Sedlak, Arkadiusz Goral, and Ireneusz Janczarski had not yet published their works, which paved their way—indirectly—for studies on phenomena that are considered paranormal but that have a definite physical basis.

The Joasia Gajewski phenomenon falls precisely into this category. When the initial manifestations occurred, the girl was thirteen years old, in the typical phase of early puberty. In her case, however, this phase was marked by a number of peculiar features.

In April 1983, when I went to Sosnowiec for the first time along with the late engineer Feliks Ilaczewski, we performed a series of experiments with Joasia. These included Manczarski's telepathy test with graphite cubes; measurement of the girl's body temperature (before, during, and after the experiments); controlled movement of a stream of potassium permanganate in a flask filled with water; discharge of 1.5 volt cells; bending of spoons and other metal items; movement of ping pong balls floating on water; observation of the perspiration process while the girl carried out certain activities; measurement of the difference in potentials between the palms as well as resistance in the skin of the fingertips; and study of her blood acidity and alkalinity. I should point out that we chose individual tests on the spur of the moment, whatever the situation called for. We sought to collect material that would be useful in later intensive analysis of the phenomenon. My preliminary observations, though, did allow me to formulate some concrete conclusions.

Q. What conclusions?

A. Let's start with a few elementary facts. Man is a thermo-dynamic system fueled externally by energy and internally by the process of respiration. In other words, he represents a definite system of biological reactivity operating on the principle "stimulus/reaction." At the same time, he lives in a biosphere consisting of an enormous number of such systems, which differ in complexity, physical structure, and states of excitation. All the constituent elements of the biosphere are centers of excitation characterized by internal transformation of matter and energy. As a result of these transformations, the systems (centers) produce certain force fields that interact with one another in a dynamic manner, leading to the creation of a definite, dynamic equilibrium. Let's call them "fields of interaction," without going into their physical characteristics for the moment.

Man is a colloidal medium consisting of structures with varying degrees of complexity and excitation. He is a medium composed of substructures (nucleotides, polypeptides) and structures (cells, tissues, organs). At the same time, he consists of the same elements as the whole biosphere. Some of them, such as salt, magnesium, phosphorus, potassium, sulfur, chlorine, cobalt, nitrogen, and iron, are structurally stable; others, like clay, titanium, nickel, arsenic, strontium, and chrome, are unstable. Finally, the body contains certain trace elements that impart specific, discrete features to the centers of excitation (e.g., helium, lithium, beryllium, argon, scandium, gallium, radium, germanium, lead, wolfram, gold, mercury, and selenium).

Metabolism is man's state of excitation as a colloidal medium, whereas the "fueling" process can be likened to the action of stimuli affecting the formation of the organism's basic structures. Metabolism is nothing but the process of internal transformation, which results in the phenomenon of energy excitation accompanied by emission. Emission, in turn, represents the external effect of all the interactions occurring in the human organism. It used to be called the aura; today the concept of "biofield" is more common. For my part, I believe it would be best to speak here of human fields of interaction, for they have the characteristics of force fields and a medium of information.

All this clearly shows that man, by virtue of his reactivity (or to be more precise, selectivity), functions as a director of stimuli (signals) he either generates himself or receives from the environment in the form of information and energy. The informational component of individual reactivity may sometimes be manifested in phenomena considered paranormal, such as clairvoyance, telepathy, etc. In Joasia Gajewski's case, our tests revealed she had this very type of spontaneous, idiosyncratic reactivity.

Q. In the several talks we've had, you emphasized Joasia's specific cellular metabolism, which results among other things in highly unusual transformation of functional potentials. You pointed out the importance of such studies as measurement of body temperature, differences in potential between the hands, resistance of the skin (especially on fingers), and analysis of blood acidity. Could you explain why these studies would be necessary?

A. One significant aspect of Joasia Gajewski's case was the readings (up to 43°C) on the thermometer we used to measure her body temperature, even though she had no signs of fever. We also observed that she did not perspire when she became fatigued after increased physical exertion. The first instance would seem to indicate the thermal effect of a magnetic field affecting the mercury; the latter instance—the retention of water and sodium by her body. Like potassium, sodium in the presence of chlorine becomes an active element "transporting" energy. It readily combines with oxygen. The combination of sodium and water releases thermal energy, hydrogen, and sodium hydroxide. Sodium also has the capacity of self-induction and is characterized by the low ionization energies of three electrons. Moreover, the half-life of its isotopes is 2 years, 6 years, or 15 hours respectively (for magnesium and neon). This generates excitatory energies as well as large amounts of hydrogen, which is not "burned off" in metabolic processes and which consequently gives rise to a special emission.

One of the most notable features of this emission is the acoustical effects occurring in Joasia's presence. To simplify matters somewhat, they can be compared to the effect obtained in the laboratory when a hydrogen or carbon electron is "knocked out" of orbit. However, the kinetic effects manifested as spontaneous movement of objects around the girl are the same as those that probably occur in antigravitational conditions.

Finally, the bending of spoons and other metal items by rubbing, and the breakage of aluminum flatware are due, in my opinion, to the differentiated dislocation of electrons in the structure of matter, which permits changes in their very network.

Metals, we should explain, comprise a network of positive ions in electrical gas. Introduction of a definite quantity of energy increases the energy of electrons over the barriers of potentials. As a result, during individual phases of this state, Joasia's metabolism presumably generates tunnel phenomena known to quantum physics. Such phenomena, which normally occur at low temperatures, involve penetration of particles through the barriers of potentials in a manner inconsistent with classical physics.

Q. Recently the psychokinetic phenomena around Joasia are beginning to take new forms, such as water dripping from her apartment ceiling in various places even though damage to the plumbing has been ruled out. How do you account for this?

A. The dripping indicates that a chemical reaction is occurring: OH (a hydroxide radical) + H^+ (hydrogen) yields H_2O (water), and H_3O^+ +OH yields $2H_2O$, whose constituents derive from radiolysis of water. Joasia Gajewski, as a generator and detector of certain electrodynamic and thermal waves, may induce those reactions.

Q. Do you believe the disturbances are generated by the girl's entire body or only by specific parts of it?

A. In the course of our research and observations, we found that these effects happened whether Joasia was sitting, lying, or standing, but they were concentrated at the level of her head. For example, during one experiment, a glass of tea on a table in front of me (the girl was sitting on the floor just then, so her head was more or less at table height) suddenly began to "undulate" (an effect similar to the waviness of air over heated asphalt). A second later, it disappeared with a loud bang (implosion). At that very moment, we realized, the glass had flown into a wall and shattered to bits.

Q. Do you think there's any chance the girl can consciously control these phenomena? This question relates to the previous one: Do you see any possibility of generating such effects for research purposes (under laboratory conditions, for example), and if so, how?

A. The observations made up to now show that the kinetic effects occur when Joasia is at least temporarily relaxed and free of inner tensions, which she has no lack of. (We should remember that the physical damages caused by flying objects naturally have a stressful impact on the teenager.) On the other hand, because she's eager to demonstrate her abilities in the presence of a large number of observers, who are not always well-disposed, Joasia may "freeze up" mentally. As a result, such tests usually end in failure.

Q. Many independent, impartial witnesses (persons outside the family) confirm that objects have passed through walls. It seems utterly fantastic, but there's considerable evidence showing this really happened (such as accounts by eyewitnesses in late January-early February 1985 at a sanatorium in Zakopane). Does physics have an explanation for this phenomenon? Or can it be explained at all—except by referring to miracles?

A. It's not necessary to fall back on miracles. We only need to picture the elasticity of the electrons and bonds comprising matter (one example is the so-called magnetic memory relating to spatial form) to accept the possibility of these effects.

Let's use our imagination for a moment. The phenomenon in question involves the passage of one solid medium through another. Now, the structure of a solid body is such that the particles forming it are distributed over a fairly large area (relative to the size of individual particles), and the structure as a whole is "glued together" with electrons. Although the electron's structure is unknown (particularly the one-third of its mass not converted into energy), the recognized models permit dynamic filling of the electron with intermittently displaced elementary particles. The variability of their energy, motion, path, and shape determines the elasticity of the bonds, and under certain conditions passage may become possible.

Q. Do you think the kinetic effects that have been occurring around Joasia for more than three years will cease at the end of puberty, or will they continue?

A. Some of these phenomena definitely disappear at the end of puberty, usually a year afterward. If they do continue, however, they may take a dangerous form. From the information you've given me, it appears Joasia is getting hurt more often lately by pieces of flying glass. I believe this indicates the presence or aggravation of stress or neurotic states in the girl that are changing the nature of her biofield. Unfortunately, the prognosis in such a case isn't favorable.

By way of consolation, I'd like to say that anyone with a high degree of psychic sensitivity can control receiving and generating specific stimuli. This involves the gradual development of the ability to restrict and fine-tune the signals received. This ability can be developed if one has at least a general understanding of the phenomenon's mechanism. That's the basis of yoga, various types of meditation, and other techniques for altering consciousness. Advanced adepts, especially those from the Far East, can unfailingly attain a state of relaxation (incorrectly termed concentration). In this state, they neither see nor hear normal stimuli but do experience other visual and auditory impressions. They're able to isolate themselves at will, even for half a minute. If Joasia were to master this skill, which is so common in countries of the Far East, I think it might significantly reduce and mitigate the kinetic effects.

A Specific Transfer of the Cerebral Hemispheres
An Interview with Dr. Miroslaw Harciarek

Miroslaw Harciarek (b.1950 in Sosnowiec) has a PhD in psychology. He explores the functioning of the cerebral hemispheres by using afterimages and specializes in the treatment of neuroses. As a staff member of the Institute of Psychology at the University of Silesia, he was on the team investigating the Joasia Gajewski phenomenon. Currently he is a lecturer in the Department of Psychology at the Academy of Physical Education in Katowice, and also has a private practice (hypnotherapy, individual psycho-therapy, etc.).

Q. Is it true that when you were given the opportunity to join the team studying the Joasia Gajewski phenomenon, you had many reservations and were openly skeptical toward its existence?

A. Yes, that's right. I first learned about the phenomenon from a TV news report, which piqued my curiosity. I concluded it would be wise to approach the case in a strictly scientific man-ner. The attempts by the "experts" on the TV program to explain it seemed simplistic, especially as they referred to radiesthesia, which itself requires explanation. I thought the mystery could be solved with psychological studies.

Q. So the stories about your skepticism were exaggerated?

A. You misunderstood me. I was simply convinced that the factor "responsible" for the telekinetic effects lay in the mental realm, which not only did not rule out a hoax but made it one of the most plausible hypotheses. If it did turn out that trickery was involved, I would be interested in finding out who was behind it and why. But if we were dealing with a real phenomenon, it would be fascinating to delve into Joasia's mind.

Q. What happened next?

A. A couple of days later I got a phone call from a colleague of mine, who urged me on behalf of Dr. Eustachiusz Gadula at the hospital in Repty to conduct psychological studies on Joasia. He said a team of experts was being assembled to investigate the Gajewski case, and the only thing they lacked was input from a psychologist.

During this conversation, I realized that the resources at my disposal were very limited, particularly the few standard psycho-logical testing methods, which would not be much help in such a situation. The studies were to be done at the Central Rehabilitation Hospital in Repty. Since many specialists were to participate, I thought I would have little time and not be able to use even the methods available to me. I was also intimidated by the scope of the project and the prospect of meager results. I told all this to my colleague, adding I would just be willing to analyze the case from the perspective of Jungian psychology. But to accomplish this, I'd need more time than I anticipated would be offered to me in Repty. And so, after weighing all the pros and cons, I at first declined.

Then my colleague replied: "You're doing research on afterimages; you could study the girl with your equipment." In fact, I was researching afterimages, studying their occurrence in various persons, but had never dealt with subjects who exhibited psychic powers. Nonetheless, this last argument swayed me and I finally accepted the proposal.

Q. The record of the initial experiments with the girl at the Repty hospital shows you remained skeptical for a long time…

A. Indeed, I would describe my attitude toward the case then as hypercritical. This was primarily because I'd never witnessed the psychokinetic phenomena generated by Joasia, and the accounts by other persons seemed vague and unconvincing. I was particularly suspicious about the quickness of those effects — they reminded me of a goblin's pranks. The eyewitnesses hadn't actually seen anything except the outcome: broken glass and streaks of liquid splashed on walls. Thus, it's no surprise we had serious misgivings with regard to the operation of psychic forces. Another explanation seemed much simpler and more plausible.

Q. Yet step by step you finally overcame your initial resistance. How did that come about?

A. I decided to concentrate on analyzing Joasia's mind instead of trying to determine whether the phenomenon associated with her was real or imaginary. I know from Jung's experiments that attempts to debunk or disparage these phenomena lead nowhere. I remember in particular the story of a female cousin of Jung's who had psychic powers. Because of a hasty decision, Jung probably lost a promising subject. During his experiments, he caught the girl "fudging" and was so upset he discontinued further studies on her, thinking she was a fake.

Eventually it turned out she likely did possess such powers but was unable to channel them; not wanting to disappoint the scholar, she had decided to perform "miracles" on her own. Jung didn't realize his error until years later, when his cousin contracted a strange illness that caused her intellectual development to regress. She died at a young age with the mental level of a small child.

My skepticism toward the Gajewski case did influence to some extent the methodology of my research project, which I planned to carry out in two phases: (a) collection of data from standard psychological tests so that we could draw up a profile of Joasia in comparison with her peers; (b) studies aimed at shedding more light on the girl's possible psychokinetic abilities.

Q. What did you succeed in accomplishing?

A. Our project ran from May 1983 to the end of 1984, with slight intervals. I decided not to schedule more than three tests a day, mainly because the results might be affected by the girl's fatigue. In order to evaluate the results more accurately, I also had Joasia's parents take part in some of the studies, including the MMPI.

Here's a list of the standard psychological tests administered to Joasia:

1) Wechsler-Bellevue Intelligence Scale
2) Raven Test
3) Benton Test
4) Graham-Kendall Test
5) Lateralization Test
6) Rubenstein Pictogram
7) Kraepelin Test
8) Couvert Test
9) MMPI
10) Rorschach Test
11) Murray's TAT Test
12) Szondi Test
13) Color Pyramid Test
14) Luscher Test

15) Rozenzweig Test
16) Koch Tree Test
17) Sacks-Sidney Sentence Completion Test
18) Witkin's EFT Test
19) Strelau Temperament Inventory
20) Eysenck's MPI Test
21) Gough and Heilbrun MPI Test
22) Cattell Self-Report Inventory
23) Thurstone Temperament Scale
24) "What are You Like?" (after Choynowski and Skrzypek)
25) Stein's Psychological Self-Portrait
26) Spilberg's Self-Assessment Inventory
27) Taylor's Manifest Anxiety Scale
28) Wolpe's Fear Stimulus Inventory
29) Willoughby Inventory for Self-Assessment of Anxiety Reactions, in Wolpe's modified version

Q. That whole process sounds terribly complex, and let's be honest, it has little or no meaning to the layman.

A. I know. My aim, quite simply, was to gather preliminary data which might be of some value in compiling Joasia Gajewski's psychological portrait. While the information we obtained didn't contribute any new insights into psychokinesis, it served as a starting point for more concrete hypotheses and allowed us to compare the girl's test results with those of other children in her age group. After completing our initial task, we did an extensive interview covering Joasia's entire life history and her family dynamics.

Q. Can you briefly summarize your findings?

A. As far as the standard psychological tests are concerned, no significant deviations from the norm were found. Therefore, our personality assessment couldn't single out which of Joasia's mental traits is related to psychokinesis. We only managed to formulate general guidelines for subsequent research.

On the other hand, the sensory and lateralization tests all indicated that future studies should be designed in such a way as to help us better understand the functioning of the girl's cerebral hemispheres. This was an important finding, since many earlier researchers on psychic phenomena associated them with the functioning of the hemispheres, particularly the right one.

Here I made use of my own experiments with afterimages. These are visual images that arise from stimulation of the optic system, such as the colored spots one sees after looking at the sun. The connection of afterimages with the functional asymmetry of the cerebral hemispheres is twofold. First, afterimages are conditioned by the activity of the cerebral hemispheres; and second, from what we know about the relation between the eyeballs and the hemispheres, when examining afterimages in the left or right eye we indirectly study the functioning of the individual hemispheres. Using afterimages to explore the workings of the brain also seems relevant because with special techniques we can ascertain the transfer of stimuli between the two hemispheres. This can't be accomplished with other methods.

Q. Did you discover anything peculiar?

A. The results of studies on the afterimages in Joasia's eyes show heightened activity in her right hemisphere. The afterimages it produced were multicolored and clearly differentiated, whereas those in the left one were less differentiated, often fragmentary, momentary, and usually achromatic. I should mention that other people do not exhibit such pronounced asymmetry, that is, such a great discrepancy between the afterimages of the left and right hemispheres.

Q. What do you conclude from this?

A. When I examined the girl's afterimages with a different method, I found that those from the right hemisphere lasted longer, which is typical of normal individuals. At the same time, however, I made a finding that must be considered quite extraordinary:_there was an intensive transfer of afterimages from the right to the left hemisphere, but not vice-versa. It was four times greater than normal […] This can be interpreted as tension stemming from the joint activity of the hemispheres, with the tension moving from the right to the left hemisphere.

Analysis of these results as well as previous studies on patients in a psychiatric ward enabled me to propose a comprehensive model of brain activity, which I termed the transistor model of the joint activity of the cerebral hemispheres. It accounts for so-called psychic energy. This may be understood on the one hand as a subjective sensation of the psychic energy required for action, and on the other hand as a force observable in the form of effects a given subject generates through his actions or presence. According to this concept, psychic energy stems from the joint activity of the hemispheres, and the transistor model is the mechanism for generating psychic energy. The nature of this force, however, remains an open question.

Another remarkable finding relates to chromatic afterimages. To illustrate what I mean by this term, let's take the following example. When we look at a green circle for thirty seconds and then shift our eyes to a white sheet of paper, we see a red circle on it. This is a chromatic afterimage. The colors that such images have are complementary to the colors of the stimuli producing them, which means that a red stimulus produces a green afterimage, a yellow stimulus–a blue afterimage, and vice versa. But in Joasia Gajewski's case it turns out that only a single form of chromatic afterimage appeared–red, generated by a blue stimulus. Red, green, and yellow stimuli did not produce afterimages. The red afterimages, moreover, were not complementary, for a blue stimulus ought to produce a yellow afterimage. I should note (to cite Goscimierz Geras) that a shift in complementary colors, such as a blue stimulus gaining a red afterimage, occurs in people with a malfunctioning thyroid gland.

Q. The medical studies did not reveal anything wrong with the girl's thyroid.

A. Then the finding becomes even more intriguing, especially if we bear in mind that chromatic afterimages, contrary to orthodox views, are connected not only with the functioning of the eye itself but also with the energy processes occurring in the neurohormonal system and with the activity of the cerebral hemispheres. It's claimed that hormonal substances, by dissolving asymmetrically in both hemispheres, cause a differentiation in their activity, which leads to their functional asymmetry. The asymmetry and energy processes of the hemispheres determine in turn the chromatic afterimages. Consequently, *study of after-*

images can be looked upon as investigating the energy processes occurring in the brain.

Q. Do you mean that Joasia's chromatic afterimages may reflect her mental processes?

A. That's exactly what I think. But the matter doesn't end there. Analyses done by Ewa Panek confirmed that the girl had certain hormonal anomalies. The level of dopamine in Joasia's urine turned out to be very low relative to the norm. This finding was very important, for variations in the amount of dopamine in the body are closely associated with mental processes. Researchers studying the biochemistry of the brain had noted long ago a lower level of dopamine in the brain during epileptic seizures, and a higher level in the case of schizophrenic symptoms. Hence the results obtained in Joasia Gajewski's case pointed to a clinical picture of epilepsy.

Q. Does that mean you consider psychic phenomena a form of epilepsy?

A. That I don't know. But it does seem interesting that epilepsy is also related to the functioning of the cerebral hemispheres. Incidentally, some types of epilepsy are treated surgically by cutting the corpus callosum uniting the hemispheres, whose joint activity is so vital for the energy processes in the mind.

Q. Experiments with Joasia Gajewski also included studies on her cognitive processes and language…

A. They likewise indicated a close relationship between the processes in the girl's cerebral hemispheres and the functioning of her nervous system. For example, it turned out that Joasia's verbal associations for noun stimuli denoting objects subjected to psychokinesis can be described as "inhibited." They were usually repetitions, diminutives, or a form of the same word. These associations referred to the phonetic aspect of the given stimulus, not to its content.

Q. Why is that significant?

A. Analysis of the associations shows that words denoting objects subjected to psychokinesis were excluded from the youngster's conscious mind and repressed in her subconscious. The results of our studies can be correlated with the workings of the cerebral hemispheres to the extent that the conscious mind is connected with the functioning of the left hemisphere, and the subconscious mind with the functioning of the right. The semantic field of words that denote objects subjected to psychokinesis, and that are probably in the left hemisphere (which is linked more closely to language and speech), was controlled by the right hemisphere, or the subconscious.

Q. In light of these studies, then, do you believe the phenomenon is real?

A. Our finding that the girl has a semantic field connected with kinetic effects controlled by her subconscious proves to me that the phenomenon does exist. I rule out the possibility of trickery on Joasia's part during these studies, especially as she couldn't have had any idea what they were aimed at. The results confirmed her genuine psychic abilities and encouraged me to conduct further studies.

Let me add that one more factor indicating the reality of the phenomenon is Joasia's age. She began to manifest psychic powers when she was thirteen, at a time crucial for development of the cerebral hemispheres and neurohormonal processes. Studies have demonstrated a close relationship between these phenomena.

Q. Did you also consider the whole matter from the viewpoint of psychoanalysis?

A. Of course. After thoroughly acquainting myself with many details pertaining to Joasia and her family, I found a neat correlation between the psychokinetic effects and the family situation. According to this approach, psychokinetic attacks symbolize the girl's need for a closer relationship with her father as well as the difficulties she has in relating to her mother. Thus, psychokinetic phenomena reflect the girl's emotional state.

Q. Can such a psychoanalytic approach be reconciled with views on the functioning of the cerebral hemispheres?

A. Yes, if we agree that the subconscious is connected with the right hemisphere, and the conscious mind with the left. Then psychic phenomena would result from the special connection between the conscious and subconscious mind, that is, from the specific interaction of the cerebral hemispheres. Psychokinesis here simply represents the projection of an Oedipus complex, for example, and the activity of the hemispheres is nothing but a mechanism for reifying this projection. The joint activity of the hemispheres may also be understood as a Jungian interplay of archetypes, which the founder of depth psychology termed "syzygy," or divine harmony.

Q. What would you propose in lieu of a standard summary of our conversation?

A. I think the Joasia Gajewski phenomenon should be carefully investigated by psychologists, neuropsychologists, psychopharmacologists, physicists, and psychoanalysts. There is every indication that psychic phenomena are related to fundamental patterns of brain activity. It's also likely that substantial progress in understanding the mind and nervous system will be achieved only when we have studied psychic phenomena. They may well prove to be the key to and link between many scientific problems and disciplines. I would connect the future of this research with an analysis of the activity of the cerebral hemispheres, or to be more precise, with holographic concepts of brain functioning.

Appendix 2

A NUCLEAR PHYSICIST CONDUCTS AN EXPERIMENT

During the Third Polish National Symposium "Psychotronics 85" held in Warsaw in September 1985 and attended by guests from the USSR, the United States, West Germany, France, Greece, Czechoslovakia, and other countries, an amazing event happened. One of the speakers, who had brought along a paper titled "Pilot Studies on Psychotronic Effects on Liquids," did not present it verbally but instead showed a half-hour film illustrating his report.

The numerous spectators in the auditorium watched scenes that were near-miraculous. They saw how participants (students in Budapest schools) in a carefully planned experiment set in motion a thin metal plate floating on the surface of a liquid by simply holding their hands a short distance away from the liquid. Some of them stopped the metal plate or propelled it in the opposite direction. All of this would have seemed to be mere special effects, a sham, were it not for the fact that the author of both the report and the filmed experiment was Hungarian nuclear physicist Dr. Gyorgy Egely at a Budapest institute.

During our interview with Dr. Egely he gave us a copy of the paper summarizing the highly interesting results of his research. We think they merit some attention.

Dr. Egely launched his experiment not as part of the regular studies he conducts at the institute, but rather as a private project. Having long followed reports on psychic phenomena (more as an observer than as a believer in them), he decided to verify whether it might be possible to develop a simple and foolproof method for generating psychokinetic effects. Earlier he had studied the available literature on this subject, particularly works by Julius Krmessky of Czechoslovakia. Krmessky had described a series of experiments in which various objects were set in motion by what he considered to be psychokinesis. In Dr. Egely's opinion, those experiments, albeit intriguing, failed to answer the fundamental question: What was the causative mechanism of the recorded psychokinetic effects, and what was the simplest way to produce them?

After much reflection, Dr. Egely decided to devise his own experiment. To this end he constructed a special testing apparatus consisting of a petri dish placed under a cube-shaped glass cover [...]At the same time, pieces of wood or plastic whose thickness was equal to the depth of the petri dish were laid on either side of the glass cover enclosing the petri dish. During the experiment the subject rested his hands on them for support. To eliminate the difference in electrical potentials that sometimes occurred, the supports were covered with a thin metal mesh and connected to each other with a metal strip.

A network of coordinates was drawn under the dish to facilitate observation of a metal plate floating on the liquid. Originally Dr. Egely had debated whether to replace the metal with a drop of a dyed solution, which would have enabled him to follow the movement deep within the liquid. But he abandoned this idea because of technical difficulties: water and a dyed solution have the same specific weight. In addition, the dye dissolves and vanishes after a while, and the water itself would need to be changed frequently owing to the loss of contrast.

Dr. Egely constructed the whole apparatus in such a manner as to exclude any factors that might skew the experiment, particularly air currents. He also wondered if the movement of the liquid could be affected even by involuntary trembling of the hands. He devised tests to eliminate this possibility.

Dr. Egely took special care to minimize the effect of possible electrostatic phenomena on the outcome of the experiment. (Incidentally, even if they had occurred, the effect would have appeared immediately in the movement of the metal plate when the subject's hands were above the water.) During the experiments, however, the radial movement of the liquid and the floating metal plate, which Dr. Egely called the "marker," usually did not commence until several minutes later.

The researcher also decided to eliminate any possibility that movement of the marker might be caused by a temperature difference, which would skew the measurements. He used three aluminum containers, whose temperature he monitored while filling them gradually with water. The measurements showed that the greatest movement of the metal plate under these conditions was 30 degrees. It occurred when the containers were being filled quickly with water [...] But when the water was poured in slowly and carefully, the metal plate did not move. Although the initial temperature of the liquid reached 52°C, in the final phase of measurements (6 minutes later) they dropped to 20°C.

Dr. Egely explained to us that with a liquid having a surface area of 200 cm^2, with an average hand temperature of 40°C, and with an ambient temperature of approximately 20°C, thermal power amounts to some 8 watts and produces only a slight air current. This is due to the fact that the space where the heat exchange occurs is just a few centimeters, resulting in a low coefficient of heat penetration. Therefore, the researcher was certain that heat transfer could not have been a meaningful factor in the experiment.

We have gone into great detail to explain the conditions under which these studies were conducted because the general criticism of such experiments is that they fail to eliminate the effect of factors other than psychokinesis in registering a phenomenon. In the case of Dr. Egely and his collaborators, we believe these requirements were fully satisfied.

Dr. Egely commenced his experiments in 1982 with twenty students during the preliminary phase. These initial measurements were not documented. Only later did he conduct experiments with a larger number of people under controlled conditions that enabled him to precisely record his findings.

The most important experiments were carried out in February and December 1984. About 300 people took part. During the initial phase the subjects were usually high school students aged 14-17 (most often girls); in the second phase, they were students in the drama department of an acting school.

Dr. Egely recounts: "First, we briefly explained the purpose of the experiment to the participants and showed them the proper way to hold their hands. We also asked them to concentrate as hard as they could but said it would be no problem if we failed to obtain results. Then the subjects were brought in groups of five to the interview room, where we recorded their personal data: name, age, academic level, favorite course in school, grade in physical education, and how tired they were feeling at that moment. Once this was completed, they proceeded individually to the testing room, where the person conducting the experiment checked the position of their hands and observed the floating marker. When it started moving, a stopwatch and a camera were turned on. The camera operated automatically for ninety seconds."

Owing to a shortage of film and the need to economize, only those parts of the experiment were recorded in which the psycho-kinetically induced movement of the metal plate on the liquid was clearly visible. According to those conducting the experiment, this usually happened within two or three minutes. The camera was not turned off until the plate moved at least thirty degrees. The experiment was considered a failure if the change in position amounted to less than 30 degrees or if no movement occurred at all.

Returning to Dr. Egely's account: "The results of the experiments in December 1984 were as follows: *almost half* [our emphasis] ended successfully. The distribution of results was uneven, however. First, we filmed the participants who had done well previously in such an experiment at home—after initial preparation. Nearly all of them managed to repeat it. The next group, the majority of the subjects, were those who had never undergone such tasks before. Their rate of success varied. The worst results were obtained [...] when the tests began early in the morning. All the students complained of sleepiness. Thus eight tests, one after another, ended in failure—this was unprecedented. After a while the weather cleared up, the rain stopped, and the sun came out. The students felt less tired. More of the tests turned out successful, although the results were still not very good. Around two o'clock in the afternoon, the subjects started to complain of fatigue again, and their performance deteriorated.

"In February, when we tested the same participants, the results were much poorer. But the measurements were made the day after the school dance, which had lasted until the early hours of the morning. The particularly harsh winter was probably a contributing factor as well. The extremely low temperature—minus 25°C—had a bad effect on everyone. In this situation only one experiment in ten was successful, and the markers generally moved about 30-60 degrees, whereas in the previous series we had observed movement at a rate of 360 degrees a minute. We therefore conclude it is highly probable that fatigue has a considerable, if not decisive, effect on the operation of psychokinetic forces."

The most intriguing results were obtained in the next series of experiments, in which students from an acting school took part. Dr. Egely's interest in them was not accidental. As he explained, to get into that school they had to pass competitive entrance exams, which in itself indicates they were superior students. They had listed poetry, drama, music, and history as their favorite subjects. Only one of them had an interest in physics. This group of students cooperated eagerly in the experiment and were generally "easy-going and open-minded." As far as psychokinetic effects are concerned, they achieved the best results.

Dr. Egely continues: "In some instances, the markers moved not in regular circles but in irregular curves. We noticed that the deviation occurred mainly when a marker came near one of the hands. It's curious [...] that, regardless of the position of the hands [two different positions were used in the experiments], the direction of the movement was usually clockwise, but sometimes also counterclockwise. What's more, when the initial movement of the markers was generally counterclockwise, their direction quickly reversed. We were most surprised to find that in two instances the movement was exclusively radial: the metal plates moved apart toward the sides of the container. Their distance from each other was too great to attribute to surface tension. We did not film these cases because we thought we had made a mistake. Not until later, when subjects produced the same effect many times, did we conclude that this was no error but a real psychokinetic effect, only of a different kind. We can simply designate them as static cases in contrast to the others, which we termed dynamic. I should add that in some cases we observed a very regular circular movement. This is clearly visible in the film."

An essential postscript: After entering the testing room, all the participants placed their hands on a grounded radiator to eliminate static charges. In the second series of experiments, the subjects' hands were measured and their temperature was taken. Although the measurements of their hands ranged from 100 to 200 cm², the recorded temperature hovered around 32°C, with the greatest difference (plus or minus) not exceeding 3 degrees.

Of course, Dr. Egely's film *Bioelectricity* shown at the "Psychotronics 85" symposium in Warsaw could present only snippets from the many weeks of experiments. The first segment featured control tests involving thermal and electrostatic phenomena. Then the action of the Lorentz force was demonstrated in a strong magnetic and electrical field. The final, longest part of the film featured the psychokinetic experiments themselves, in which one could see how the water in the petri dish and the markers floating in it began to whirl slowly under the effect of the subjects' hands.

The project's findings surpassed all expectations. Out of the three hundred people who participated in the experiments, ten percent were successful. In other words, thirty individuals achieved results indicating psychokinetic action. As Dr. Egely put it: "Having eliminated any factors that might affect the outcome of the experiments, we concluded that the recorded movement was obviously due to psychokinesis."

The Hungarian physicist told us he intended to expand the scope of his research in the future. Among other things, he would like to determine to what extent a subject's vision affects the outcome of tests, i.e., whether visual feedback is necessary for obtaining psychokinetic effects. Up until then only a single experiment had succeeded with a blindfolded subject. Dr. Egely thought it would also be advisable to conduct studies in which participants do not know the expected result (in which case they would just be taught how to hold their hands). Finally, it might be worthwhile to repeat similar experiments, e.g. by using gloves or barriers made of different kinds of material.

Dr. Egely's findings support one overall conclusion: psychokinetic phenomena are not quite as rare and elusive as we commonly assume, and they certainly have nothing to do with supernatural properties of the living organism.

Suggested Readings

Ashford, Jenny. *The Unseen Hand: A New Exploration of Poltergeist Phenomena.* CreateSpace, 2017.

Ashford, Jenny, & Mera, Steve. *The Mammoth Mountain Poltergeist.* CreateSpace, 2015.

Ashford, Jenny, & Mera, Steve. *The Rochdale Poltergeist: A True Story.* CreateSpace, 2015.

Clark, James & Hitchings, Shirley. *The Poltergeist Prince of London: The Remarkable True Story of the Battersea Poltergeist.* The History Press, 2013.

Clarkson, Michael. *The Poltergeist Phenomenon: An In-depth Investigation into Floating Beds, Smashing Glass, and Other Unexplained Disturbances.* Weiser, 2011.

Fraser, John. *Poltergeist! A New Investigation into Destructive Haunting.* 6th Books, 2020.

Gauld, Alan & Cornell, Anthony. *Poltergeists.* White Crow Books, 2018.

Goss, Michael. *Poltergeists: An Annotated Bibliography of Works in English, Circa 1880-1975.* Scarecrow Press, 1979.

Healy, Tony & Cropper, Paul. *Australian Poltergeist.* Paul Cropper, 2014.

Henderson, Jan. *The Ghost That Haunted Itself: The Story of the McKenzie Poltergeist.* Mainstream Publishing, 2001.

Houran, James & Lange, Rense (eds). *Hauntings and Poltergeists: Multidisciplinary Perspectives*. McFarland, 2007.

Lecouteux, Claude. *The Secret History of Poltergeists and Haunted Houses: From Pagan Folklore to Modern Manifestations*. Inner Traditions, 2012.

Matthews, Rupert. *Poltergeists: And Other Hauntings*. Arcturus, 2018.

Maxwell-Stuart, P. G. *Poltergeists: A History of Violent Ghost Phenomena*. Amberley Publishing, 2012.

Nandor Fodor. *On The Trail of The Poltergeist*. Literary Licensing, 2011.

Playfair, Guy Lyon. *This House is Haunted: The True Story of the Enfield Poltergeist*. White Crow Books, 2011.

Ritson, Darren. *Poltergeist Parallels and Contagion*. White Crow Books, 2021

Ritson, Darren. *The South Shields Poltergeist: One Family's Fight Against an Invisible Intruder*. The History Press, 2020.

Rogo, D. Scott. *On the Track of the Poltergeist*. Anomalist Books, 2005

Roll, William G., & Storey, Valerie. *Unleashed: Of Poltergeists and Murder, The Curious Story of Tina Resch*. Pocket Books, 2007

Roll, William G. *The Poltergeist*. Paraview Special Editions, 2004

Summerscale, Kate. *The Haunting of Alma Fielding*. Penguin Books, 2021.

Tucker, S. D. *Blithe Spirits: A History of the Poltergeist.* Amberley Publishing, 2020.

Willin, Melvyn J. *The Enfield Poltergeist Tapes: One of the most disturbing cases in history. What really happened?* White Crow Books, 2019.

Wilson, Colin. *Poltergeist: A Classic Study in Destructive Hauntings.* Llewellyn, 2009.

INDEX

Itoh, Yoshihiro, 54, 57

Jach, Jan and Gertruda, 3-5
Jagiellonian University, 14, 42, 83-85
Janczarski, Ireneusz, 13, 133
Japanese Society for the Study of Extrasensory Perception, 46
Joasia (pronunciation of), 1
Judge F., 94-96

Kapitsa, Pyotr, 111
Katowice, 65, 66, 139
Kiyota, Masuaki, 103
Kociecki, Maciej, 108-109
Kolak, Krystyna, 68-69, 71, 74-75
Konin, 92
Krakow, 39, 42, 71, 83, 85, 128
Krakow Nuclear Research Institute, 39, 83, 85
Krasnystaw, 106
Krmessky, Julius, 149-150
Kubis, Gerard, 82-83, 92
Kudry family, 93
Kurier Polski, 14
Kuznik, Grazyna, 93
Kyota, Matsuaki, 14, 62

Lasota, Leszek, 103

Lodz, 45, 46, 93
Lodz School of Engineering, 45
Logunov, Professor, 115-116

Madry, Topor, 75
Manczarski Test, 12, 133
Manczarski, Stefan, 132, 133
Matin, Boguslaw, 49
Matsumoto, Teruo, 61
Matura, Artur, 93
Maxwell, 115, 116, 119-120, 123
Meandry fizyki, 114
Mereshvili, 115
metabolism, 132, 134-136
metallography, 29, 45, 46
microvibrations, 40
Miners Medical and Vocational Rehabilitation Center No. 1, 11, 27, 29, 49, 51
Ministry of Health and Social Welfare, 29, 46-47, 51, 53, 67, 83, 128
Myszkow, 93

Nakaoka, Toshiya, 46
Newton, 116
Nieznany Świat, 109
Nobel Prize, 104, 131
Nuclear Research Institute, 39

www.ingramcontent.com/pod-product-compliance
Lightning Source LLC
Chambersburg PA
CBHW060854280326
41934CB00007B/1040